CW00542072

MG
A PICTORIAL
HISTORY

John Tipler

with photographs from
The National Motor
Museum, Beaulieu

CROWOOD

First published in 1995 by
The Crowood Press Ltd
Ramsbury, Marlborough
Wiltshire SN8 2HR

British Library Cataloguing-in-Publication Data

A catalogue record for this book is available from the British Library.

ISBN 1 85223 923 9

Printed and bound in Great Britain by BPC Hazell Books Ltd
A member of the British Printing Company Ltd.

Contents

A History of MG

Apart from Rolls Royce, MG is probably the best known marque in the world. But unlike the majority of manufacturers who started from scratch when the industry was in its infancy, MG emerged from the production-base of an established make as the sporting by-product of worthy but relatively unexciting cars. Its seventy-year history has ranged from the heady peaks of competition success – spurred on by individuals like Cecil Kimber, John Thornley, Syd Enever, and Marcus Chambers – to depressing troughs of badge-engineering when it was the toy of corporate whimsy. The advantage of corporate ownership is that the cars have frequently been equipped with reliable drivetrains and running gear, sourced from more mundane vehicles, which has brought practical sports-car motoring to a broader spectrum of ownership.

In the early 1920s, in the optimistic aftermath of the Great War, Morris Garages was a dealership in Longwall Street, Oxford selling the output of Morris Motors' Cowley factory: Oxfords and Cowleys. A fierce price-cutting contest was in full swing at the time, led by Morris Motors as they successfully courted the mass-market customer. The price of a four-seater Cowley was slashed by £100 to £425 in 1921, and sales more than doubled in a year with 6,937 units sold. By 1925, sales had hit 54,000. Unmoved by such commercial considerations, Morris Garages' manager, Cecil Kimber, sought a more exalted level of operation. He commissioned a small run of close-coupled four-seater bodies from Coventry coachwork specialists Carbodies, and fitted them to Morris Cowley chassis at the Morris Garages premises. They were marketed as the Morris 'Chummy'. After a short time the 'Chummy' operation was relocated at workshops in Alfred Lane, still under the auspices of Morris Garages, and Kimber set about producing a run of six tourers using a body made by local coachbuilder Charles Raworth – who had made two-seater bodies for Morris at least ten years earlier. The first vehicle to be advertised as an MG was a four-door saloon, based on the Oxford chassis and called the MG V-front Saloon. It was advertised as such in the March 1924 issue of *The Morris Owner* magazine, pre-dating an advert for the Raworth-bodied two-seater by just two months. Catchline for the latter was 'The MG Super Sports Morris', the words set in the now-famous octagonal surround, and the Raworth-bodied model should be considered the first of the line since a yellow one was sold on 11 August 1923 – to a certain Oliver Arkell for £300.

Modifications to regular Morris cars included lengthening the wheelbase of the Oxford, which was exploited stylistically by Kimber with a short run of sporting four-seater cars in the latter part of 1924. Kimber's special talent was to improve the handling of standard models by modifying spring rates, dampers and steering rake, as well as fitting a higher final drive ratio, calculated to make his cars more attractive to the sporting motorist. When Morris dropped the 'Bullnose' (an abbreviation of Bullet-nose) radiator shape in September 1926, Kimber followed suit, for the 1912 Bullnose look was by now very dated.

Production was difficult in the cramped confines of the Alfred Lane workshops, and in September 1925, Kimber's operation and its fifty-strong workforce annexed part of Morris Motors' radiator workshop at Bainton Road, Oxford. This was simply a prelude to Morris Garages being set up as a limited company in July 1927, and renamed the MG Car Company (Proprietors of Morris Garages Ltd) in April 1928. It is significant that William Morris – later Lord Nuffield – retained ownership and he agreed to Kimber's plans for a new purpose-built factory solely for the manufacture of MGs at Edmund Road, Cowley, and supported the venture to the tune of £10,000. Although they still bore Morris chassis plates, Kimber's cars were now classified as MGs, and a degree of independence from Morris Motors was established. Building work impeded car production, and the only vehicle of note shown by MG at the Motor Show in 1927 was a Gordon England fabric-bodied Featherweight Saloon, based on a Morris Oxford chassis.

Until 1928, MGs had started out as Morris rolling chassis. But now, Kimber's production methods began to change as he sourced components from manufacturers other than Morris. While a Cowley chassis frame might still be used, the rear axle might, for example, come from Wolseley. Now each model had its own manual too. MG production for 1928 totalled 300 units, and this was trebled the following year with the introduction at the Olympia Show of the 2.5-litre 18/80 Sports Six, and the MG Midget, running an 847cc ohc engine sourced from the Morris Minor; it is no coincidence that both these power units owed much to Wolseley, as the company had been acquired by Morris the same year, but MG practice included the polishing of induction and exhaust ports and combustion chambers, and fitting stronger valve springs to improve performance. Pride of place on the MG stand was taken by the 75bhp 18/80 Sports Six, however, as it was built to Kimber's own chassis design and could comfortably out-perform the Alvis Silver Eagle and 3.0-litre Lagonda Six.

The introduction of the Midget was significant as it paved the way for the entire line of small MGs which have featured so prominently in the marque's dynasty. *The Autocar* magazine proclaimed that the Midget, with its boat-tailed plywood body and lowered suspension, would 'make sports car history.' More than half MG's output for 1929 was comprised of Midgets, with most of the remainder made up of 18/80s and a small proportion of the older 14/40 model. Midget production would make MG the largest sports-car builder in the world. The Mk 2 18/80 now came with a substantially strengthened chassis, and Kimber began to develop the engine for a works competition car. Pistons and crank were changed, a cross-flow twin-plug head was fitted, and the result was the Mark 3 18/80, known as the Tiger, which debuted at the Brooklands Double Twelve event in 1929.

With Cecil Kimber as managing director, the next major step in the MG saga was the move to Abingdon-on-Thames – then in the county of Berkshire – in 1929. The plant had outgrown the Edmund Road works, and was moved some seven miles out of Oxford to premises belonging to the Pavlova Leather Company. It was a bold move, for the country was on the verge of a severe recession – as indeed was most of the 'western world', and sales dipped below 1,500 units in 1931. MG weathered the depression and sales picked up the following year to 2,400. Although the factory was 'out of town', the showroom was at Queen Street, Oxford.

THE GOLDEN AGE

Meanwhile, Kimber's sporting programme was paying off, with successes for MGs as far afield as Buenos Aires in 1927 – when Alberto Sanchiz Cirez took first place in a one-hour event driving a 14/40, and in numerous trials, sprints and minor race meetings. As early as 1923, Kimber's own special bodied trials car had been a prizewinner in the Lands End Trial, and another leading late 1920s triallist, Billy Cooper, drove an MG – which was frequently parked by the timekeepers' box at Brooklands where it attracted a lot of attention. The kudos gained through competition success is unquestionably good for sales. *The Autocar* road tested an MG in its 25 May issue in 1925, and both *The Motor* and *Motor Sport* magazines had greeted the marque with enthusiasm.

A bewildering succession of Midgets, Magnas and Magnettes followed, prefixed by a seemingly impenetrable code of type letters and numbers, and to add to the confusion, a combination of body styles, engines and chassis were common to different models. These were indeed the halcyon days of MG, witnessing the real flowering of the marque, and by 1933 MG enjoyed sufficient charisma to attract to its pit counter none other than the great Tazio Nuvolari, who took his K.3 Magnette to first place in that year's Ulster Tourist Trophy at Ards. Earlier that year, MGs had won the team prize with first and second places in class in the Mille Miglia, Italy's stupendously challenging road race. Using a single-seater version of the K-type Magnette, Ronnie Horton broke lap records at Brooklands in 1934 and further demonstrated MG's superiority with a Midget – the smaller car being only marginally slower around the banking.

Kimber had, up to a point, still to toe the line, as the company continued to be owned by William Morris, an anti-racing man. No matter what consequent benefits accrue in the sales showroom, racing is a costly business, and Kimber was urged to kerb such expenditure. His response was to drop the Carbodies coachwork and use in-house creations instead, but such economies were all for nothing, as in 1935 William Morris transferred the MG Car Company back under the jurisdiction of Morris Motors. Enter Leonard Lord, future boss of Austin and later BMC, who as managing director of Morris Motors, saw fit to close down the MG competitions department. It was an economy measure carried out in the wake of the costly modernization of the Morris Motors plant, and rationalization of its somewhat irrational model range. MG's efficient ohc engines were also sidelined in favour of retro-engineered stock Morris and Wolseley pushrod units, so that the TA Midget was powered by virtually the same engine as the Wolseley 10 – albeit with 52bhp, plus better weather equipment and improved handling over earlier models. The 2.0-litre Wolseley Super Six engine was used to power the S.A. model, a large plush saloon, introduced as competition to the new Jaguar SS. Jaguar's streamlined production schedule saw its SS in the showrooms some six months ahead of the MG S.A.

Meanwhile, Kimber pressed on with a touring model, using Charlesworth bodies, and a drophead coupé with Tickford coachwork. MG production reached a pre-war zenith in 1937 with 2,850 units sold. The end of the decade at Abingdon witnessed a range of commodious sports tourers – the VA and WA – of mediocre performance, powered by 1.5- and 2.6-litre engines. In private hands, MGs continued to shine in competition, but Kimber's last-ditch attempt to involve the works in a sporting programme came in 1938. He persuaded William Morris – now Lord Nuffield – to buy George Eyston's EX.135 record-breaking car and fit a streamlined body designed by Reid Railton. Its 1,087cc engine was supercharged and Col. Goldie Gardner set a class record for the flying kilometre at 187.62mph (302.07km/h), raising it to 203.05mph (326.91km/h) in 1939.

END OF AN ERA

Although car production stopped when the Second World War broke out, the Morris penumbra – known as the Nuffield Organization – did not pass on any war work to MG, to the frustration of the patriotic Kimber. However, the War Ministry ensured that MG was involved, and Abingdon was soon building Crusader tanks and Neptune amphibious tanks, as well as frontal sections for Albemarle bombers and engine mounts for Lancasters, Typhoons and Tempests. Sadly, this did not go down well with autocratic Nuffield managing director Miles Thomas, as the Albemarle bomber contract had been taken on without his approval. Astonishingly, in 1941, Kimber was dismissed. He went on to work for Charlesworth coachworks and the Specialloid Piston company, getting both companies on a war footing; he was returning to London in February 1945 after a business trip for the latter when he was killed in a train accident.

After the war, the only MG in production was the TB, although it was quickly superseded by the TC, and exports to the US took off in 1947. Such was the popularity of the TC Midget that the much vaunted Sports Car Club of America grew out of one branch of the MG Car Club. By 1950, some 10,000 TCs had been built, of which 6,592 were exported, and of these 2,001 went to the States. MG TDs took the team prize in the 1952 Sebring twelve-hour race, further enhancing MG's reputation in the USA. The marque's competition heritage continued to be buoyed up by Col. Goldie Gardner's record breaking forays on the Belgian Jabbekke motor road and Italian autostrada in his ageing streamliner. Between 1946 and 1948 he claimed a number of records, including a remarkable 154.23mph (248.31km/h) over the flying mile using a 497cc MG engine. He took a new car powered by a 213bhp TD engine to the Bonneville salt flats, Utah, in 1951 and 1952 where he set further records. Stirling Moss took the single-seater streamliner EX.181 to Bonneville in 1956, and running a 1.5-litre twin-cam, recorded 245.64mph (395.48km/h). Another Grand Prix star, Phil Hill (World Champion in 1961), took the same car to 254.91mph (410.40km/h) in 1959. The 1950s was a decade much preoccupied with out-and-out straight-line speed, and as the age of jet propulsion advanced it was natural that records were set and broken by all types of vehicle.

Back on the production line, the Y-type four-door saloon of 1947 provided the basis for the TC's successor, the TD, which used a shortened Y-type chassis. The TD was made in far greater numbers than previous MG sports cars, as production methods improved, and nearly 30,000 units had been built by 1954.

The downside of corporate ownership began to make itself felt again, when Leonard Lord turned down the plans for an all-new Midget because of the introduction of the Austin-Healey 100; in his opinion, a second sports car was counter-productive to the marketing plans of the newly-formed British Motor Corporation. Another side to this was the advent of badge-engineering, which saw several models from companies within the Corporation sharing the same engines and bodyshells. Individuality was suppressed, and thus we find the 1954 MG Magnette ZA saloon clad in the same body as the Wolseley 4/44 – related stylistically and mechanically to the Wolseley 6/90, which in turn was based on the Riley Pathfinder chassis; this is unsurprising because Riley had shared the Abingdon factory since 1948 and designer Gerald Palmer (of Jowett Javelin fame) headed BMC's Cowley design team. The Magnette was unquestionably the prettiest and easily the most competent of the bunch, and the updated ZB version sold well between 1956 and 1958.

The TF roadster was the result of a face-lifted TD, shown at the 1953 Earls Court Show. The TF used largely tried-and-tested TD chassis and mechanicals, and although the more curvaceous body took the dated T-type Midget styling a stage further, it was still perceived as being behind the times, especially when compared with the contemporary Healey and TR2. The Abingdon management quite correctly saw that its future lay in the lucrative sports-car market rather than the more intensely competitive saloon-car sector, and in 1955 the MGA came out to rapturous acclaim. These cars were sleek, handled well, provided good performance and, starting with the 70bhp 1.5-litre A-series engine, the specification progressed through the next seven years with such delights as fixed-head coupé styling, the sparkling 1,588cc Twin-Cam and 1,600cc Mk II models. By 1962, 101,181 MGAs had been produced and the model had restored MG's slightly tarnished competition credibility, having been run successfully in a variety of international events, including the Le Mans Twenty-Four-Hours.

Meanwhile in 1958, Austin-Healey production was transferred to Abingdon, and the 'Frog-eye' Sprite was introduced, clearly fulfilling the role previously occupied by the Midget. The record was set straight in 1961 with the revival of the Midget nomenclature, which, like the Sprite also used the small BMC A-series engine. The new MG Midget was also the victim of badge engineering to a certain extent, as it shared the same shell and running gear as the updated Sprite.

More of the same market segmentation came with the MG 1100 of 1962 – basically a standard front-wheel drive BMC 1100 four-door saloon with an MG badge, some leather and walnut trim and a second SU carburettor, a package aimed at the would-be sporting motorist. The finned B-series Farina saloon bearing the MG badge was actually made on the Austin line at Cowley and was in no way a proper representative of the marque. It received much the same cosmetic treatment as the 1100, and was referred to as the Magnette Series III and IV. Along with the 1100's successor, the MG 1300 saloon, the Magnette was phased out by the BLMC regime in 1968.

As the production run of the MGA came to an end in 1962, MG brought out its most enduring model, the MGB. Its aesthetics were absolutely right, and its performance and handling suited exactly the requirements of the average sporting enthusiast. The range was extended in 1965 with the introduction of the equally attractive MGB GT, which also used the 95bhp 1,798cc BMC B-series engine. The similarly-styled MGC and MGC GT (with bonnet bulges and taller wheels) appeared in 1967, and were unfairly criticized for failing to match the old Austin-Healey 3000. The MGC used a redesigned version of the 3.0-litre straight-six, but its handling was never satisfactorily developed, and its effortless cruising potential was rather overlooked. Following the example of privateers like Ken Costello, the Rover 3.5-litre V8 unit was shoehorned into the MGB GT in 1973 for a short production run lasting until 1976, which again never quite fulfilled its promise.

By 1971, MGB production had passed the 250,000 mark and demand was buoyant. But the advent of US safety legislation in 1973 led to the jacking-up of the MGB suspension to fulfil light-height requirements and the fitting of rubber impact-absorbing bumpers, which effectively killed the B's good looks. Corporate politics had dealt MG a series of bad hands, from the merger with Jaguar in 1968, when the MG Car Company became simply the MG Division of British Motor Holdings, to the subsequent Leyland merger and creation of British Leyland. From then on, MGs were competing with Triumph TR6s and Spitfires from the same stable and even demoted to the downmarket Austin-Morris division. To add insult to injury, the unfortunate Midget was given the more powerful Spitfire engine so it could keep up with the competition.

In 1982 BL Cars Ltd became Austin Rover Ltd and the MG saga entered its next phase. Abingdon was never favoured by BL boss Lord Stokes or Austin-Rover supremo Sir Michael Edwardes, both of whom were keener on the higher profit-earning saloons. As a result, yet more badge-engineering ensued as the MG name suffered what many see as the indignity of identifying top-of-the-range Metro, Maestro and Montego saloons. The Montego Turbo was certainly quick off the mark, but the fact remains that these MGs were really nothing but pseudo-sports saloons. The only machine worthy of the MG badge was the mid-engined four-wheel-drive V6-powered Metro 6R4 Group B rally car, which shone briefly in the mid 1980s.

Apart from the show-car prototype EX-E of 1985, no new sports models were produced in the 1970s and 1980s. The Midget was mercifully terminated early in 1979, while the MGB soldiered on until autumn 1980, when the Abingdon plant and the Competitions Department were finally closed down. The factory was sold off by British Leyland the following year to the

Standard Life Assurance Company for £5m.

With a resurgence in sports-car popularity in the early 1990s, the MGB V8 concept was revived, fifteen years after the MGB's demise, in an unprecedented move by Rover Group. The British Motor Industry Heritage Trust had most of the tooling needed to produce the car, and the new shells were made at Faringdon, Oxfordshire, incorporating subtle styling changes to bring the B's classic shape more up to date. Thus the MGB RV8 was introduced in 1992 as a precursor of entirely new MG models to be made under the BMW regime. Enthusiasts did not have long to wait: the launch of the Rover K-series twin-cam-powered MGF in March 1995 heralded the marque's long-overdue renaissance.

Pitched somwhere between such paragons of sportscar motoring as the Mazda MX-5 and the Toyota MR2, the mid-engined, rear-wheel drive MGF is dynamically state of the art, with agile handling and excellent roadholding. Its suspension system is far more sophisticated than that of most rivals: double wishbones at each corner allied to front-to-rear Hydragas springing.

The First MGs: 14/28,14/40, 18/80, 18/100 Tigress

The MG 14/28 Super Sports was based on a Morris Oxford chassis and continued to use the 'Bullnose' radiator, which had been a Morris feature since 1913.

This 1926 MG 14/28 Super Sports four-seat tourer is finished in fashionable duotone paintwork. Bolt-on wire wheels were new for this model year and a brake servo was fitted.

The standard Morris artillery wheels of this Bullnose MG Super Sports tourer of 1925 are fully covered by discs, and fresh air is fed into the scuttle through jaunty nautical-style funnels. The radiator cap features an unusual art nouveau mascot.

Cecil Kimber powers his 'Special' up a gradient on the way to winning a gold medal at the Bluehills Mine, Cornwall, a stage on the 1925 Land's End trial. His partner here is Wilfred Matthews.

There has been some controversy as to whether or not this is the first true MG. Popularly known as 'Old Number One', FC 7900 is more correctly regarded as a Morris Garages Special, built by Kimber (posing in the car here) for competition purposes on a shortened Cowley chassis. The engine is an ohv version of the Hotchkiss-derived Cowley engine, and all four wheels are braked. Whatever its designation, its rakish lines, cockpit faring and lightweight mudguards identify Kimber's intentions more clearly than contemporary 1925 Super Sports tourers, and it has majored in MG publicity shots since being restored by the company in 1932. The car is on display in the British Motor Industry Heritage collection at Gaydon.

A 1925 MG 14/28 receives a helping hand round a tight turn on the Lynmouth trial, north Devon.

This 1927 14/40 model uses the new Morris flat-radiator style and has boat-tail bodywork by Jarvis and Sons of Wimbledon. The front mudguards are more pointed than other 14/40s and the split windscreen has opening vents. The 'flying lady' and scarab beetle mascots are also interesting additions, as is the reversed tympanum shape under the radiator, a device sometimes soldered on under Kimber's instruction to disguise the Morris-derived radiator.

The 1,802cc engine of the MG 14/28. Kimber's special tuning involved polishing the ports and combustion chambers, and fitting stronger valve springs to improve performance.

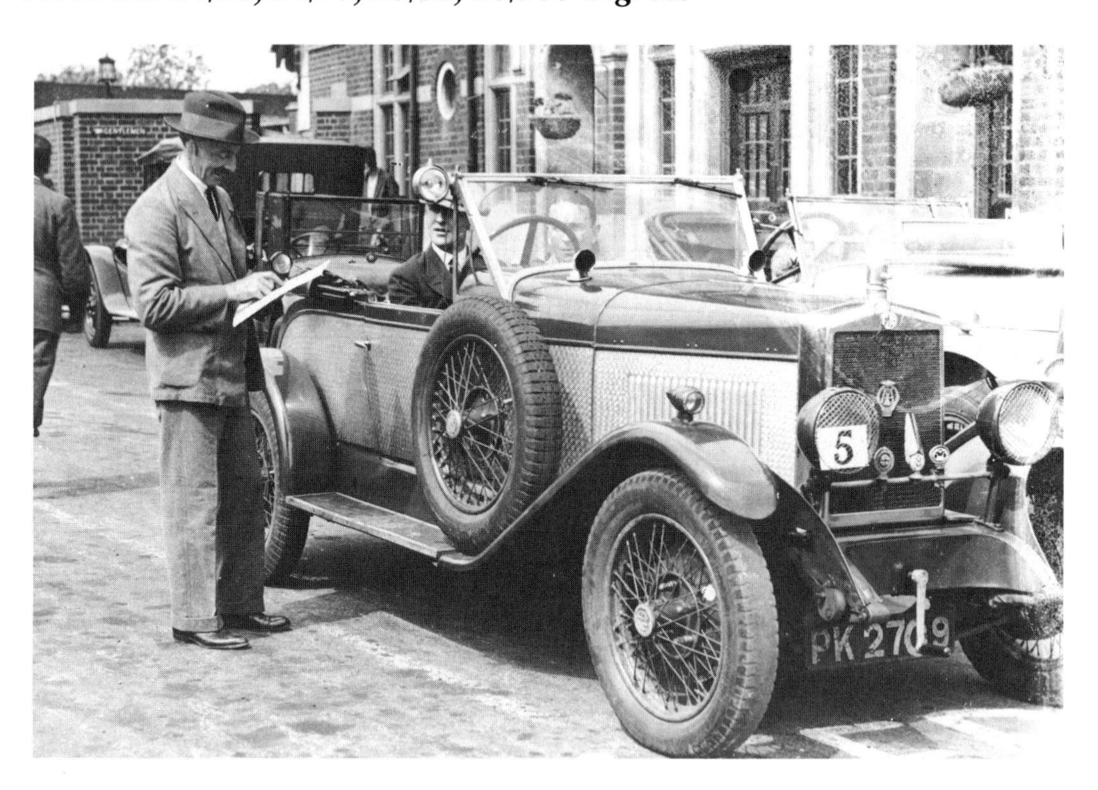

An MG 14/40 Mk IV Sports Coupé taking part in the North West London trial in 1929. Bolt-on Rudge-Whitworth racing-type spoked wheels are fitted and the headlamp lenses have mesh stoneguards.

The unpainted aluminium panelled sections on this 14/40 Mk IV Sports Coupé provide an interesting spangled finish. With the top up, it was at least showerproof.

The 18/80 Six of 1928 used a 2,468cc six-cylinder Morris engine, which had a chain-driven overhead camshaft and twin SUs, and developed 60bhp. It was fitted in the first chassis to be developed by MG and was thus a considerable advance on previous models.

A 1928 MG 14/40 out in the wilds on the West Stonedale section during the 1930 MCC London–Edinburgh trial.

This Mk I 18/80 sporting a substantial front bumper is up in the West Highlands on the 1931 Scottish Rally.

A line of Mk I 18/80 rolling chassis leave MG's new plant at Abingdon – for the draughty ride to Carbodies at Coventry.

The hustle and bustle of the Edmund Road works in 1929, as Mk I 18/80 chassis are assembled, sometimes with five men to a car.

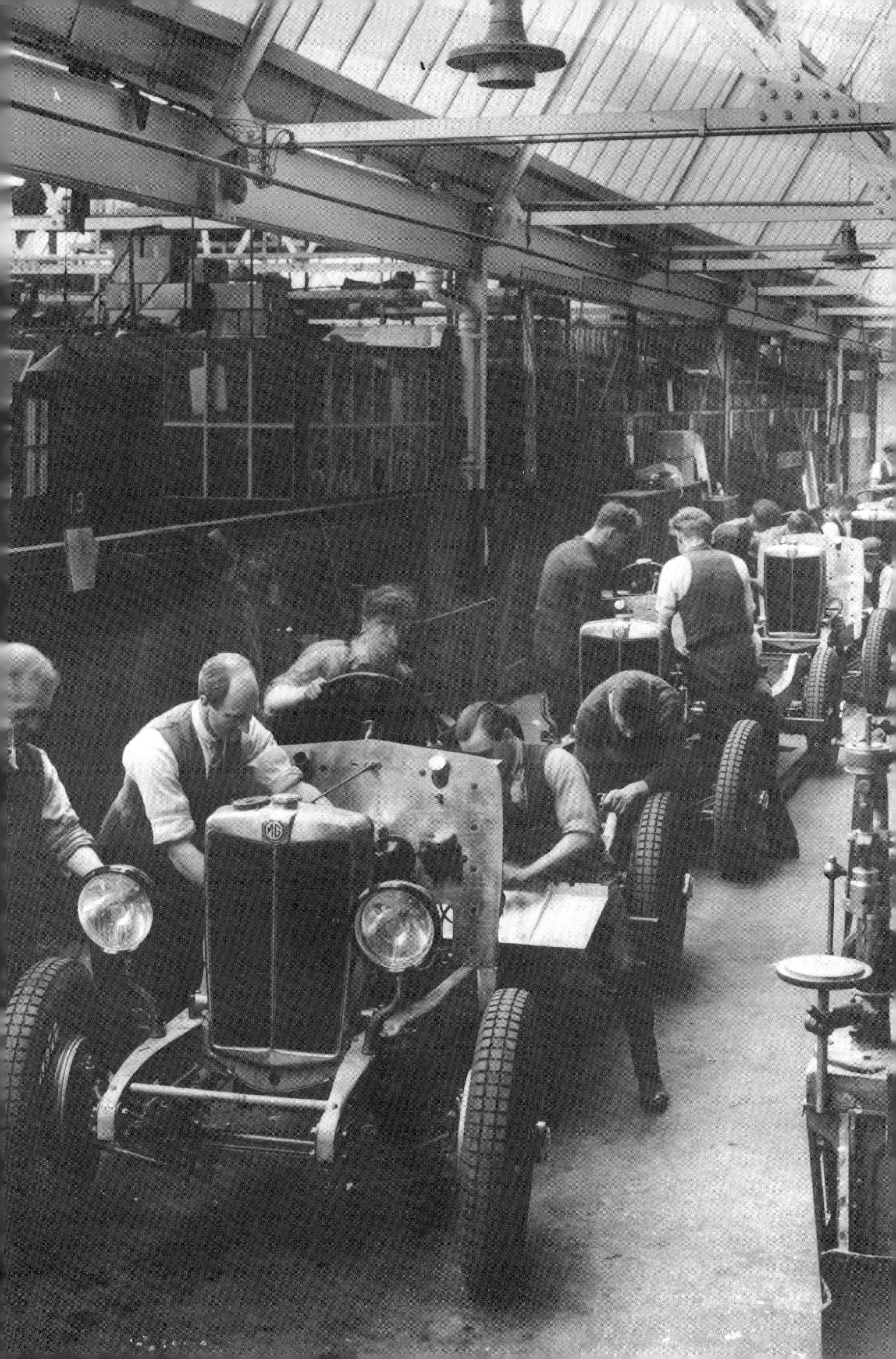
13
MG

The well-known sporting motorist Kitty Brunell about to climb aboard her Mk I 18/80 Speed model, along with two companions.

Kitty Brunell chats with a shepherd from the driving seat of her 1930 MG 18/80.

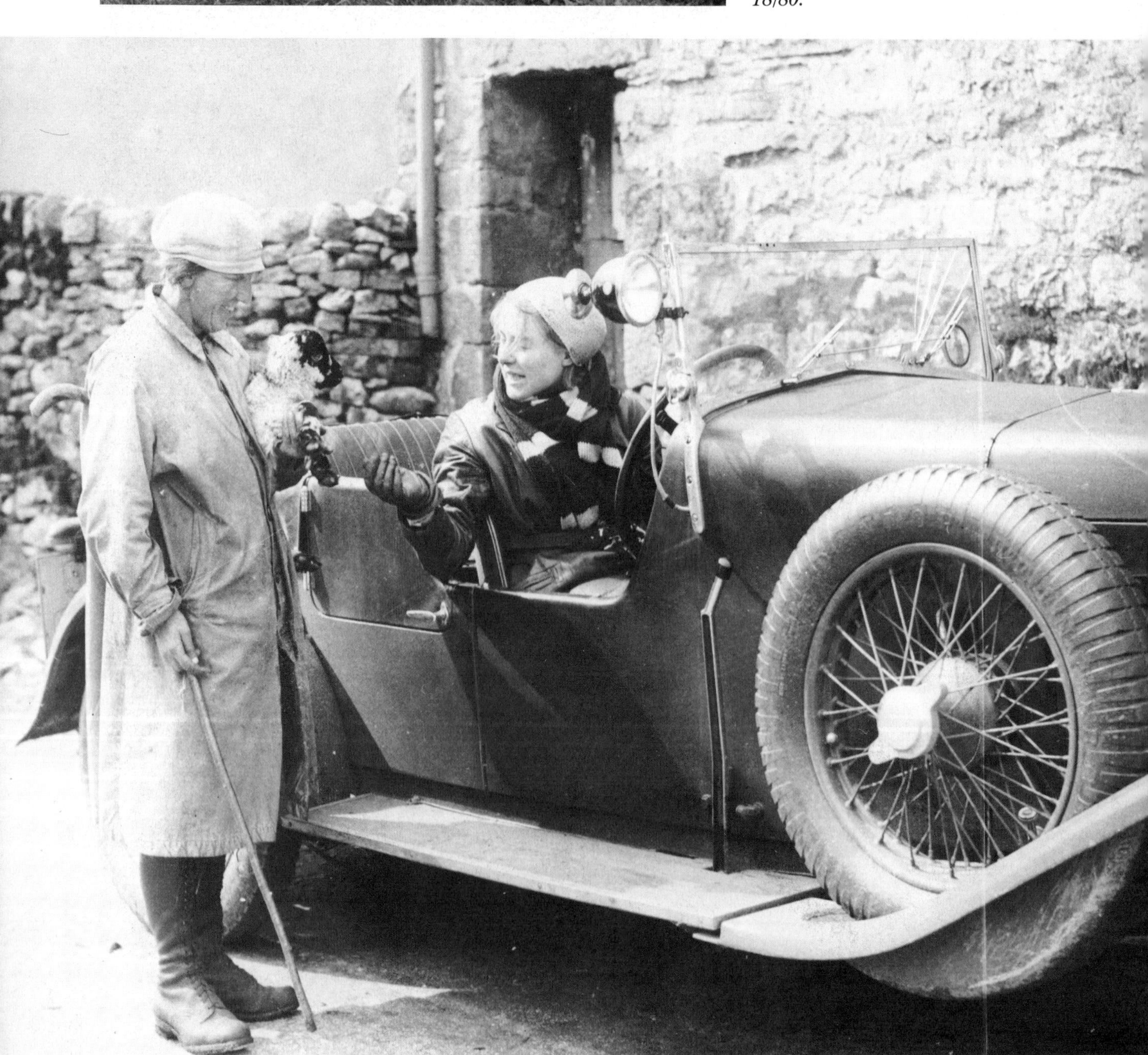

A 1930 Mk I 18/80 scales a gradient in the Bluehills Mine section during a Land's End trial in the mid 1960s.

Raincoats on in the Derbyshire Dales, as this 18/80 Mk I prepares to leave a checkpoint on the 1930 Buxton trial.

By 1930, the 18/80 had a wider track, four-speed gearbox and improved brakes, and was designated the Mk II. This 1931 model has a Weymann coupé body.

The Mk II 18/80 is most easily identified by the angled headlamp braces either side of the radiator. This one is participating in the 1930 MCC London–Edinburgh trial.

Trialling attracted considerable spectator interest, and the crowds lining this section are treated to the rather incongruous spectacle of a coach-built salonette version of the Mk II 18/80 being put through its paces.

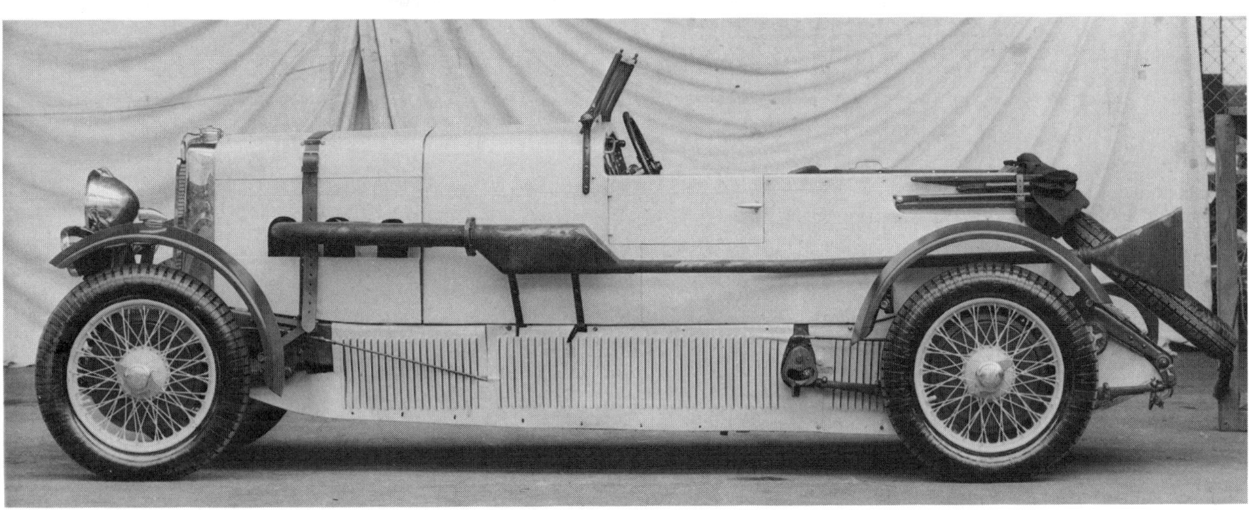

In 1930 Cecil Kimber developed a road-racing version of the 18/80 known as the Tigress. It was designated the 18/100 because engine modifications, including a re-cast block, cross-flow head, dry-sump lubrication, and a dual-circuit ignition system, raised power output to 100bhp.

The Mk III evolution of the 18/80, the 18/100, was also known as the B-type on account of its chassis prefix and its four seater coachwork – with copious louvres on the chassis side-panels – featured a single narrow door on the nearside, and a fold-down windscreen. Like contemporary racing Bentleys, it conformed to international competition regulations.

MG Midgets: The M-Type

The M-type Midget was introduced at the 1928 Motor Show and was an instant hit with less wealthy enthusiasts. It was based on the Morris Minor chassis and used a modified 847cc Morris engine, at first delivering only 20bhp.

This competitor in his M-type Midget appears to be taking a rather casual approach to the special section on the 1937 Welsh Rally.

Chas Robinson helps a lady competitor tune her M-type Midget at Brooklands. She may also have benefited from advice on her over-glamorous racing footwear – a sartorial paradox compared with the racing overalls.

On the starting grid at Brooklands in July 1934 for the JCC High Speed Trial; a pair of MGs, an M-type Midget (36) and a P-type (28) line up alongside a Riley (26).

This mud-spattered M-type Midget crew check their route on the MG Car Club's first trial.

Victoria Worsley, with her M-type Midget, set to take part in the JCC British Double Twelve Hour race meeting at Brooklands, 9 and 10 May, 1930.

The Midget was the first of MG's small sports cars, and its evolution was a four stage affair. The original M-type, shown here, was superseded in 1930 by the 27bhp Double Twelve model – named after the Brooklands event – followed by the competition C-type Montlhéry in 1931, which was available in supercharged or unblown form. The M-type remained in production through to 1932, when the longer chassis D-type model appeared, still with the 27bhp engine.

The 1930 MG Midget Sportsman's Coupé, with window panels in the roof and sliding side windows. Accommodation in the rear seat was minimal to say the least.

An M-type Midget with slightly modified grille goes 'mud plugging'.

In the wake of their team's success at Brooklands in May 1930, MG entered two Double Twelve Midgets for the Le Mans 24-Hours. Neither car lasted the distance.

Carver's M-type Midget – minus windscreen – out on the 1931 Intervarsity Hill Climb.

An M-type Midget takes a break on the inaugural MG Car Club's first trial.

An M-type turns heads without generating wild enthusiasm as it passes by on this trial section.

The driver of this 1931 M-type Midget looks for the shallowest crossing point at a ford during a summer trial.

M-type Midgets have their natty hoods put up during a wet lunchtime halt on the Land's End trial. A contemporary report in The Light Car and Cyclecar *(14 February 1930) reported that the hoods kept the elements at bay, but restricted the headroom somewhat.*

R.D. Crump's M-type Midget prepares to leave a farmyard checkpoint ahead of a Magnette and another Midget on the MCC's Buxton trial.

MG C-Types

The MG C-type Midget was fitted with special 743cc versions of the Midget engine, derived from Captain George Eyston's EX.120 Montlhéry record breaker, and clad in aerodynamic radiator cowls. C-types were immediately successful in the 750 class, taking the first five places and the team prize in the 1931 Brooklands Double Twelve race. No fewer than fourteen C-types were entered, and the winning car was driven by the Earl of March and Chris Staniland.

An MG C-type Midget is prepared for the team's successful assault on the 1931 Brooklands Double Twelve two-day event. C-types finished third in the Brooklands 500 miles, averaging 92mph (148km/h), and won the Ulster TT on the Ards road circuit and the Irish Grand Prix. Although it remains the most numerous of MG's competition cars, only forty-four examples of the C-type were ever produced.

A trio of C-types brave the heat and dust as they get away at the start of a Brooklands race.

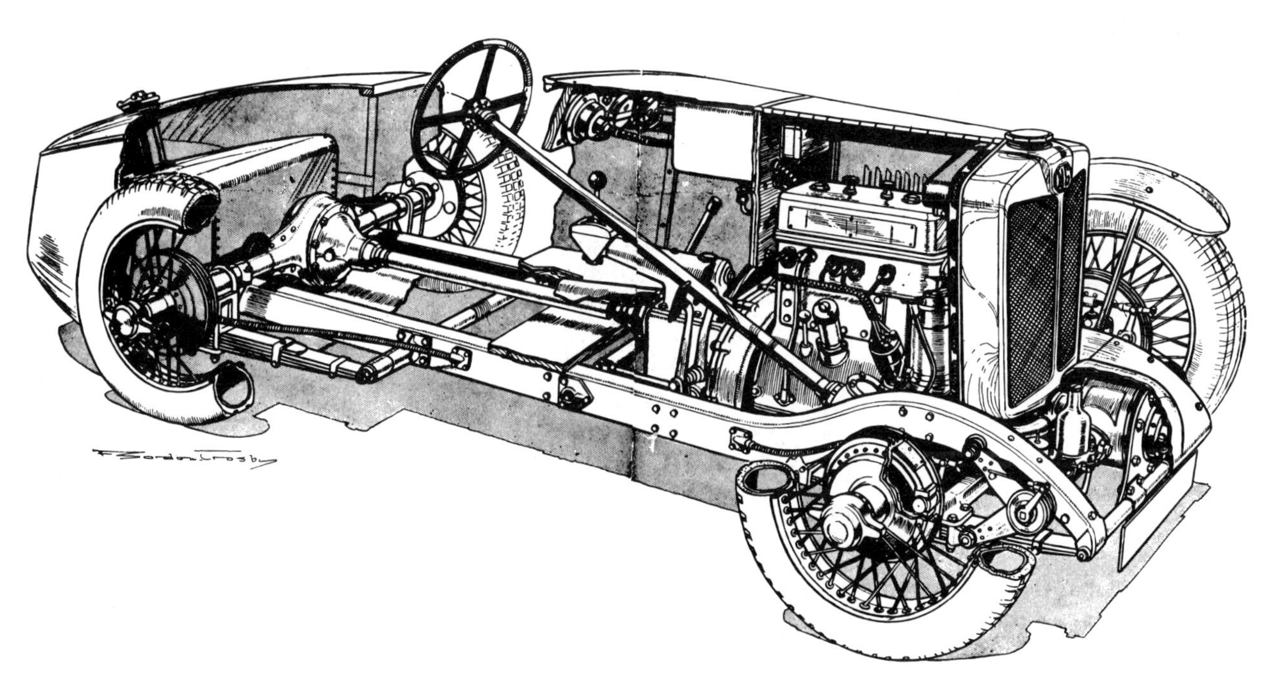

Cutaway illustration of a C-type Montlhéry Midget, showing the hefty ladder type chassis, lever arm and leaf-spring suspension system. The supercharger is housed ahead of the radiator.

One that didn't make it: a C-type is pushed back to the pits.

The vast expanse of the Brooklands banking dwarfs the field, with a C-type at the rear, but provides an excellent vantage point for 'the right crowd and no crowding'.

EX.127: The Magic Midget

MG craftsmen at Abingdon build the buck for the body panels of Magic Midget EX.127 in 1931.

The first in a line of purpose-built MG record breaking cars was EX.120, driven by Captain George Eyston. After it was destroyed by fire at the end of its 101mph (162km/h) one-hour run, Eyston drove EX.127 – the 'Magic Midget', pictured here – at 114mph (184km/h) over five kilometres on the Montlhéry circuit near Paris.

George Eyston photographed in Magic Midget EX.127 on 13 December 1932 at Montlhéry, prior to breaking the International five kilometre record at 189.474 km/h, the first time a 750cc car had come close to 120mph.

George Eyston was a big man, and it was decided to try his mechanic, a jockey-sized driver called Bert Denly, in the car in order to improve the power-to-weight ratio. Denly, who raced the car at Brooklands, tries the Magic Midget for size at Abingdon on 13 October, 1933.

By 1933, Magic Midget EX.127 had acquired an octagonal air intake and an air scoop, and the cockpit cover was more angular. Here, Bert Denly gets a push to the Brooklands pits. He blew the engine at high speed while avoiding an accident during the Junior Car Club's 500 Mile event.

Record breaking did much for national prestige as well as the reputation of the manufacturer, and MG was quick to capitalize on the kudos of the Magic Midget's success. Here the car is paraded on a float outside the Abingdon works before a promotional excursion – its wheel discs removed.

Captain George Eyston in the Humbug, otherwise known as the 'Magic Magnette'. It could be fitted with one of two bodies, depending on the competition category, and Eyston broke twelve records with it at Montlhéry in 1934. This was the successor to the Magic Midget, which had been sold in 1934 to German ace Bobbie Kohlrausch who recorded 140mph (225km/h) in the car on the Frankfurt autobahn before it was acquired by Mercedes-Benz for dissection.

MG J-Type

A J.2 Midget driven by A.W.F. Smith negotiates Roman Bridge on the 1935 British Rally.

Profile of the J.2 Midget, of which 2,500 units were made between August 1932 and March 1934, retailing at just under £200. The chassis was based on the C- and D-types and the 847cc engine now had an eight-port crossflow head, driving through a four-speed gearbox with remote shift.

A.W.F. Smith takes his 1933 J.2 Midget up Station Hill on the 1936 London–Land's End trial.

More than any previous MG, the J.2 set the general styling for subsequent MGs. In the same way as a modern classic such as the Caterham Seven, the J.2 was strictly functional. Here we see a J.2 raising the dust on the Bugatti Owner's Club Amersham Hill Climb, 1933.

The essence of trialling is steep gradients and muddy tracks – exemplified by the MG Car Club's 1939 Abingdon trial, which this J.2 appears to be taking in its stride.

Eyston's Dancing Daughters

George Eyston managed an all-female three-car team of MG PAs at the 1935 Le Mans 24-Hours, and they are pictured at Brooklands for a practice session before leaving for France.

Three C-type Midgets line up by the pits before the 1932 Ulster Tourist Trophy on the Ards road circuit, as mechanics fine-tune the engines.

Eyston's 'Dancing Daughters' – as they were known – line up to give their PA Midgets an airing at Brooklands before their successful visit to the Sarthe: all three finished the 1935 Le Mans race.

The MG team share a joke while sitting on the pit counter; Goldie Gardner, second from right, looks pensive.

Goldie Gardner's wrecked C-type lies beside the Ards circuit while the Red Cross nurses tend the injured.

MG P-Types

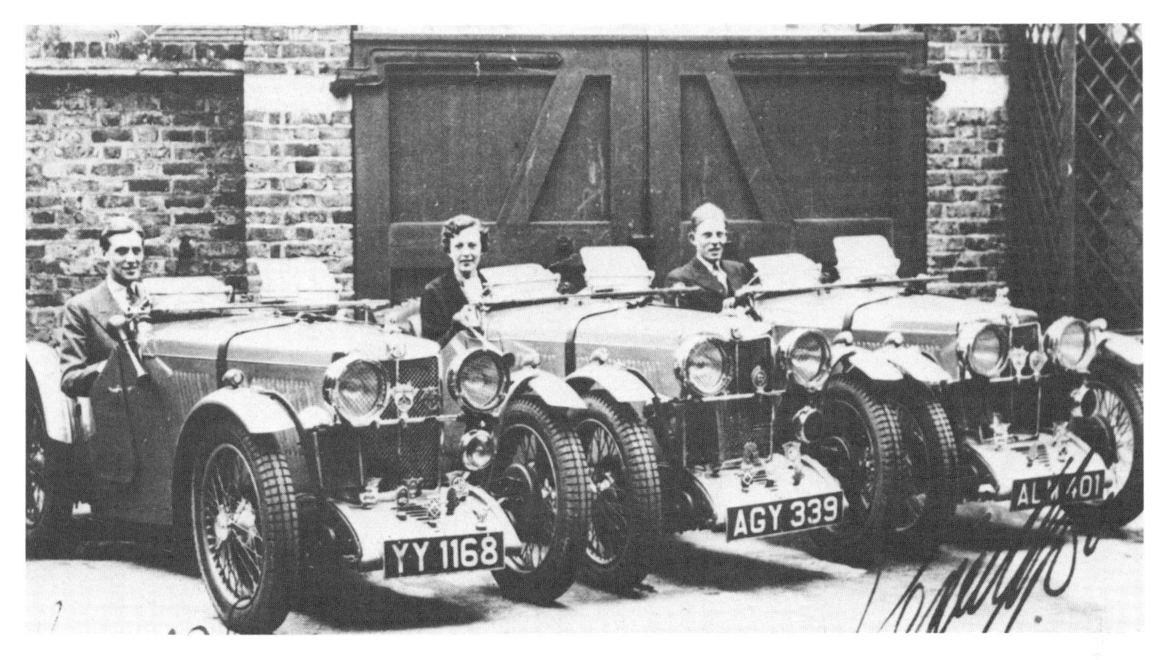

The J-type was succeeded by the P-type and was made in similar numbers between March 1934 and June 1936. The chassis was lengthened and toughened up, and the J.2 engine given a three-bearing crank. PAs were campaigned by a works-backed team comprising Jack Bastock, Maurice Toulmin and Mac Macdermid – called the Cream Crackers because of the cars' cream and brown paintwork – but were equally successful in the hands of privateers such as this well-equipped team led by Kenneth Alvary.

A P-type creates quite a bow-wave as it negotiates a ford on the Watersplash trial.

Introduced at the Kensington Olympia Motor Show in October 1934, the Airline Coupé was based on the PA chassis and cost £290. It was originally finished in grey cellulose, with silver cellulose-painted wheels, but the fashion for duotone coachwork was soon applied to its graceful profile.

Not that bloke with the red flag again! The crew of a 1935 PA with lightweight cycle-wing mudguards patiently wait their turn in a mid 1930s trial.

One of the 'Cream Cracker' PAs on the 1935 MCC Land's End trial – an event just as prestigious in its day as the current RAC Rally. The Cream Cracker cars went to the Scottish team the Blue Bustards in 1938 when the former switched to TA Midgets fitted with 1,708cc VA engines

The crowds are enthralled as the driver of this PA Midget applies full opposite lock to power the car around an uphill right-hander.

The 1934 PA of K.A. Scales gets a helping hand from spectators near Ludlow on the 1938 Midlands Sporting trial. The problem was cured and the car finished the course.

A pristine example of the 1935 PA Midget, showing the weather protection in place. It consisted of five sections, including side screens. To get a clear idea of the car's construction, it is worth seeing the cross-sectioned PA in the British Motor Industry Heritage collection at Gaydon, Warwickshire.

With MG being taken over by Morris Motors Ltd in 1935, the P-type was the last of the vintage overhead camshaft Midgets. The PB was produced from 1935 to June 1936 and differed from the PA in its dashboard layout and swept front wings and running-boards.

By 1936, the Cream Cracker team – managed by Abingdon service manager John Thornley – was using PB-type Midgets, and the distinctive colour scheme is seen here on the Lawrence Cup trial. They eventually progressed onto MG TAs powered by the bigger capacity 1,548cc VA engines.

When the PB was introduced in November 1935, it still cost £222 – no increase on the price of the PA, although the older model was reduced to clear unsold stocks. In practical terms, the main difference was the increase in engine capacity to 939cc which gave 43bhp. This PB is competing in the 1939 London–Land's End trial.

MG Q-Types

Built for competition, the Q-type Midget was a hybrid of P-type chassis and K3 Magnette body. Fitted with the new Zoller supercharger, the 746cc Q-type was basically too fast for its chassis. Between 1934 and 1936, its power output rose from 100bhp to 146bhp.

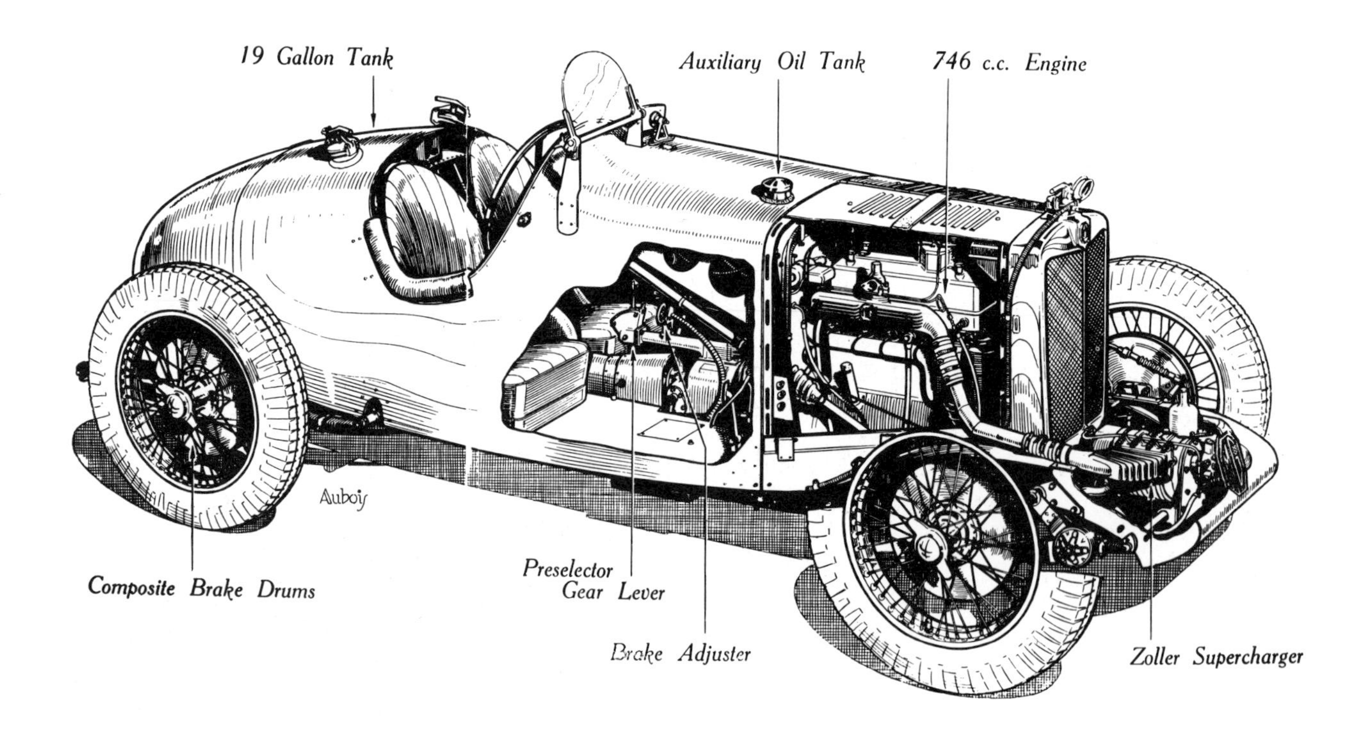

Cutaway illustration by Aubois of the Q-type Midget, identifying the major components and running gear.

The Q-type could be fitted with different bodies depending on the event it was entered for. The two-seater version seen here at Brooklands, with MG engineers alongside, has the driver on the right of the car.

The Q-type MG at this Donington Park meeting is fitted with the single-seater body.

Yet another version of the Q-type, almost a miniaturized Mercedes-Benz W25, about to take to the banking at Brooklands during the 1937 500 Miles event. Driver Noble is very much in the sit-up-and-beg position.

MG R-Type

George Eyston is to drive the R-type in the 1935 BRDC British Empire Trophy at Brooklands. It is the only MG to be built by the works as a single-seater and uses a lightweight backbone type chassis and independent torsion bar suspension. Power is supplied by the Q-type engine, driving through a pre-selector gearbox. Only ten examples of this state-of-the-art model were built, but the majority have survived.

The twin ohc 746cc Q-type engine of the R-type racer was fitted with a McEvoy–Pomeroy cylinder head, magneto ignition, and Zoller supercharger. Its power output –146bhp in 1936 – was superior to all other racing engines, worldwide.

George Eyston takes a tight line round a Douglas kerb in his R-type MG during the 1935 Mannin Beg race on the Isle of Man.

MG Magna and Magnette

The larger six-cylinder Magnas and Magnettes shared the Midget's ohc engine layout and were produced in much lower volumes between 1931 and 1936. There are strong similarities between all MG roadsters of this period, and all that differentiates the J.2 from the Magna is the latter's longer bonnet and slightly angled radiator, a likeness demonstrated by the J.2 Midget (left) and F-type Magna emerging from a ford at the Beggars' Roost section of the London–Land's End trial.

A consignment of fourteen four-seater L.1 Magnas delivered to Lancashire Constabulary in 1933. Several eminent public figures drove Magnas, including the racing driver Prince 'Bira' Birabongse of Siam, Prince Ali Khan and Earl Howe.

Kitty Brunell in her F-type 12/70 Magna on the 1932 Scottish Rally. One of the Magna's chief visual characteristics, its slightly angled radiator, is visible.

Kitty Brunell works on the 1,271cc Wolseley Hornet-derived engine of her 1932 F-type Magna.

An interesting collection of motorcycles and a Morgan Super Sports greet an F-type Magna at the summit of the Beggars' Roost – 947ft (284m) above sea level– on the London–Land's End trial

A team of F.2 Magnas, shorn of their windscreens and mudguards, won the Brooklands Relay in 1933.

The L-type Magna came out in March 1933, retaining the existing F-type track but incorporating the K.2's longer wheelbase, and featured the K.2's swept front wings. This couple are at a check point on the MG Car Club's Abingdon trial.

The Magna range expanded when the Continental Coupé was introduced at the 1933 Olympia Motor Show, although only 100 were produced. They were finished in two-tone colour schemes and remained on sale after the L-type Magna was discontinued in January 1934. This example is taking part in the 1937 Welsh Rally.

The mud flies as an L.2 Magna with cycle-wing front mudguards crests a rise during an MG Car Club trial.

An L.2 Magna takes the rough stuff in its stride during the 1939 MG Car Club Abingdon trial. The L-type Magna shares the 1,086cc short-stroke, cross-flow six of the K-type Magnette, which endows it with 41bhp.

The driver of this F.2 Magna throws it enthusiastically into a corner on the 1933 London–Land's End trial.

Pre-war Britain did not enjoy the same varied selection of race circuits as it does today, which to an extent accounts for the popularity of trialling then. Racing was held at Brooklands – unquestionably the home of British motor sport – Ards and Phoenix Park (both in Ireland – one a road circuit, the other a park), the Isle of Man, Donington Park, and Crystal Palace, south London, where this meeting is taking place. Drivers sprint for their machines in a handicap event, with an L-type Magna at centre among sundry Rileys, Singers, MGs, a Frazer-Nash and a Bugatti.

An L-type Magna follows instructions at the JCC Brookfield meeting at Brooklands, 25 March 1939.

This KN saloon's progress is reduced to walking pace; listed at £399, the pillarless saloon is said to be good for 75mph (120km/h) in The Motor*'s appraisal of 18 September 1934.*

K-Type Magnette

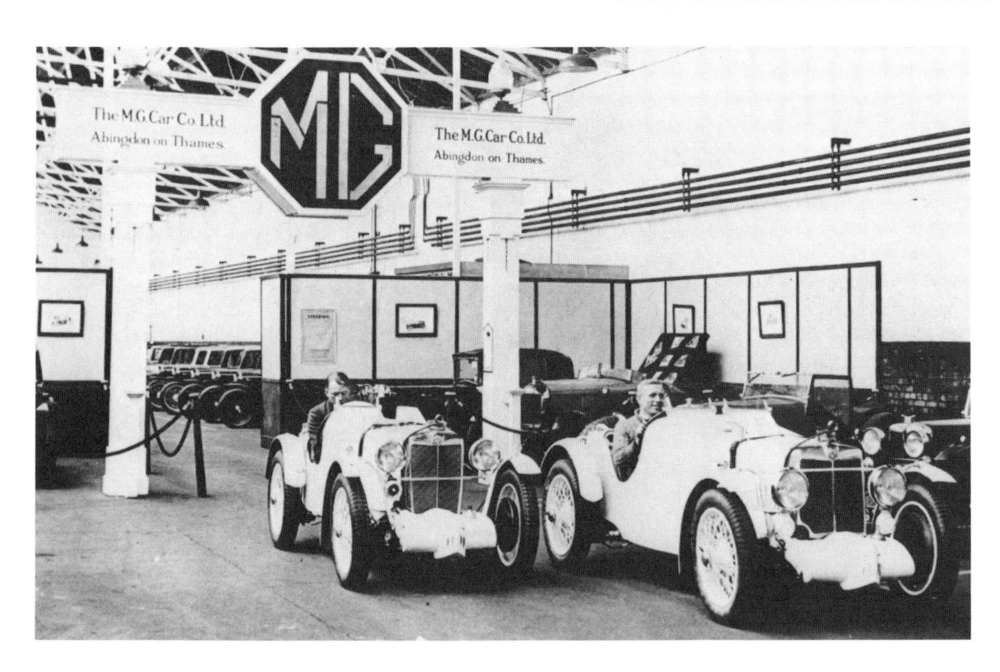

A supercharged couple at the Abingdon works: on the left is a J.4 Midget, similar to the one driven to second place in the 1933 Ulster Tourist Trophy at Ards by Hugh Hamilton, and a K.3 Magnette like Tazio Nuvolari's car with which he and Alec Hounslow won the event. Astonishingly, the J.4 was a mere 40 seconds behind the K.3.

George Eyston and Count Giovanni 'Johnny' Lurani – later an eminent motoring journalist – won their class in the 1933 Mille Miglia in this previously untried K.3 Magnette after 1,000 miles of demanding Italian road-racing.

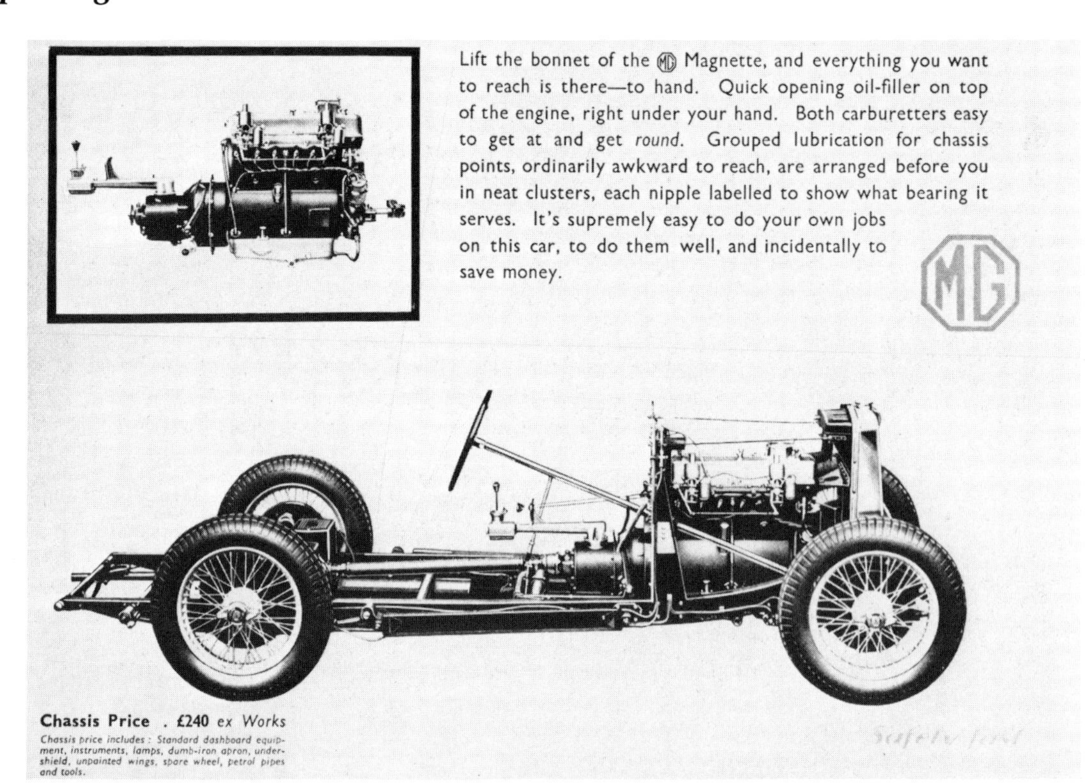

The K-type Magnette was launched in October 1932, and the chassis could accept a variety of body styles, from the KA pillarless saloon and KB four-seater drophead to the K.2 two-seater, which had a shorter chassis and a 7ft 10in (2,388mm) wheelbase. The KB engine had two carburettors, the KA had three, and there was a choice of four-speed pre-selector or crash gearbox, with remote control shift.

Probably the most significant Magnette model was the K.3, developed specifically by Cecil Kimber as an all-purpose supercharged sports-racing car. Powerplus superchargers were changed to more reliable but less powerful Marshall units for 1934 models. In the event, forced induction was banned in the TT that year, yet an unblown K.3 still managed to win the race. In all, thirty-three units were produced.

Racing a K.3 was all about bent arms and elbows, sitting close up to the steering wheel. Here Brooklands 500 winner Eddie Hall rushes up Bray Hill on the Isle of Man in 1933.

Eddie Hall's K.3 is fitted with a Zoller supercharger – like the Q-type Midget – and double back wheels for better traction. He waits for the off at a Shelsley Walsh hill climb in 1934.

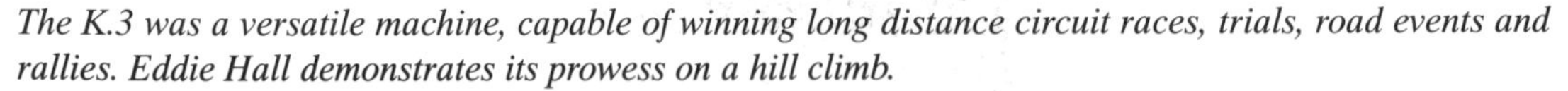

The K.3 was a versatile machine, capable of winning long distance circuit races, trials, road events and rallies. Eddie Hall demonstrates its prowess on a hill climb.

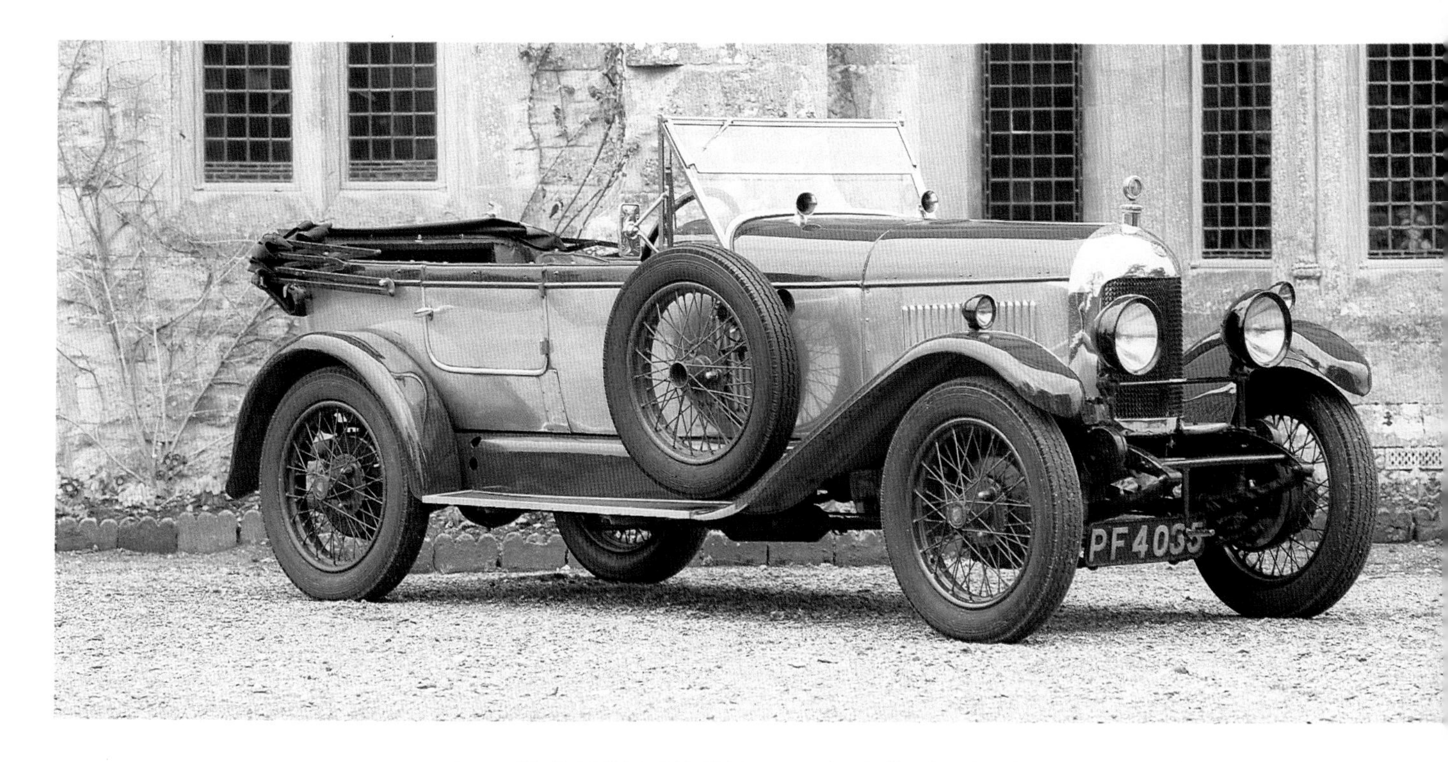

The 1926 MG 14/28 Super Sports was a sturdy four-seater, and its handsome Cecil Kimber styling owed more to the exalted Bentley tourers than to the Bullnose Morris chassis on which it was based.

Artistic elegance was used to good effect to promote the 1930 model year ohc six-cylinder 18/80. The Motor *found plenty to enthuse about in its contemporary appraisal – from fuel system and suspension mounts to its driving position and luggage capacity.*

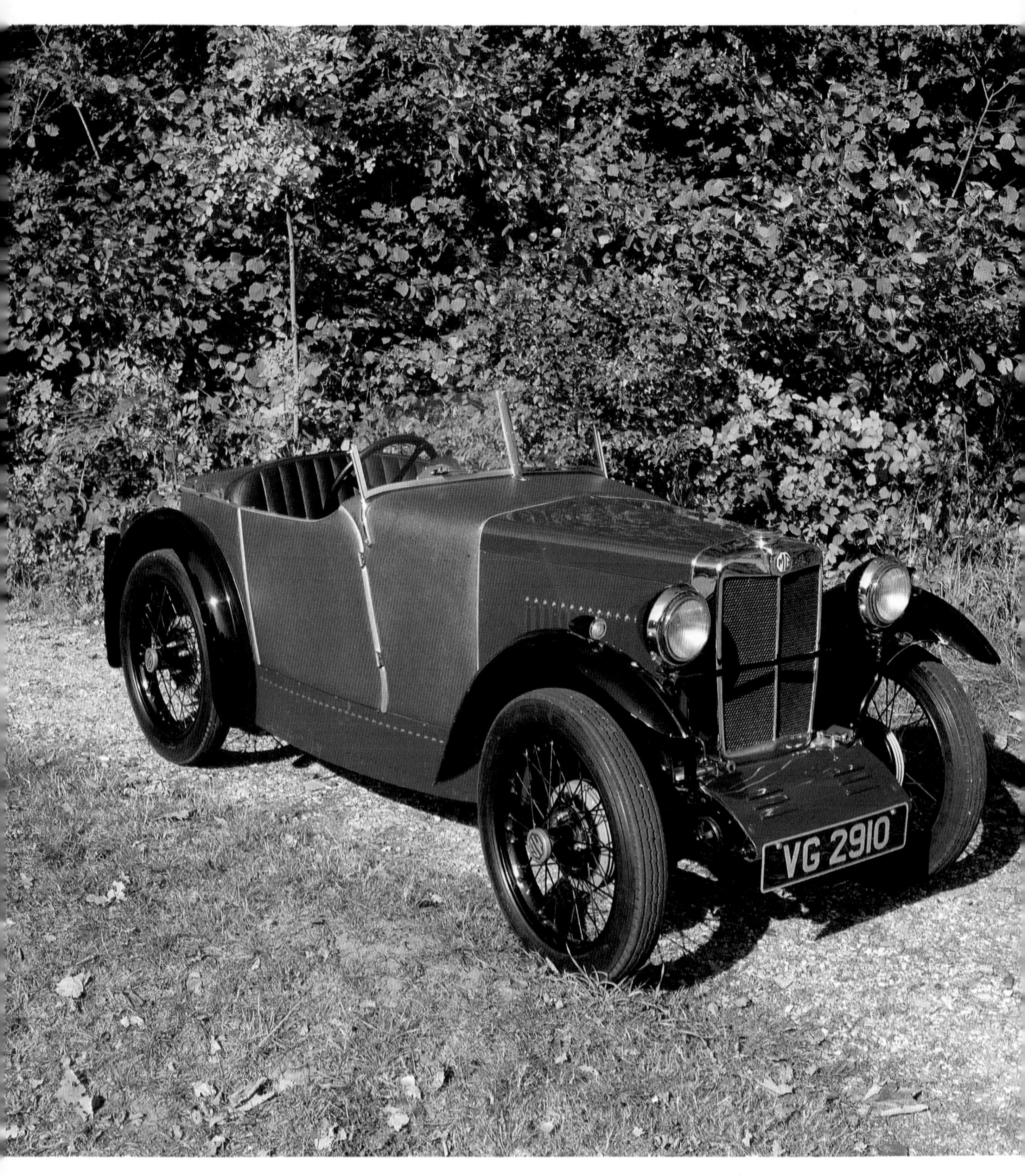

In 1930, the boat-tailed M-type Midget, pictured here, was fitted with a more powerful 27bhp engine with improved valve timing. In January 1931, The Light Car and Cyclecar *magazine praised its 'capacity for putting up good averages on the open road and appetite for hills and rough going … and docility and gentlemanly behaviour in traffic'.*

MG's promotional pic of the J-type Midget shows the car with Magna-style flowing wings and running-boards. It was more commonly sold with the cycle-wing mudguards which it would have used in competition, the model's chief selling point.

MAGNA

The M.G. MAGNA
Open Two-Seater
'L' Type - £285
ex Works

This delightful Two-seater M.G. Magna has been designed for competition work and really fast touring, and its speed capabilities make it a worthy match for any sporting company. Mechanically, this model incorporates all that racing successes have taught our designers, and the body is the last word in sporting coachwork, with its twelve-gallon rear petrol tank, cut-away doors, and streamlined scuttle. The wings, with their pleasing sweep, and the little running-boards provide ample protection from mud thrown up by the front wheels. In addition to the usual electrical equipment, the facia board contains a combined speedometer and revolution counter, eight-day clock and oil thermometer. The brakes, with their large diameter drums and well-known M.G. cased cable method of operation, more than justify the use of our well-known slogan "Safety fast!"

SECOND B.R.D.C. 500 MILES RACE

TRIPLEX SAFETY GLASS

Racing Pedigree

MG

Page Five

Cecil Kimber was keen on fishing and yachting and it is not surprising that MG's publicity material alludes to an age of sporting leisure and motoring-inspired freedom, attainable for £285 in 1933 with the low-slung L-type Magna. Presumably the fisherman is either describing the size of his catch or the extra length of the six-cylinder Magna's chassis.

SAFETY FAST!

The M.G. Magnette K3 Racing Model. Unsupercharged £595. Supercharged £695
With Pre-selector Gearbox.

THE 1933 M.G. MAGNETTE 'K' SERIES

The 1,086cc straight-six engined K3 was the racing variant of the 1933 Magnette range, sold with pre-selector gearbox in supercharged or normally aspirated form, and with a body built to international racing regualtions. It could cost between £475 in its most basic form and £695 with special equipment.

Evidently the ideal vehicle for a picnicking foursome, the K-series Magnette's superior build quality and full specification exemplified the luxury end of the light-car market segment. Because of the company's competition activities the Magnette was seen as a racing car adapted for fast touring, rather than a standard production model modified for racing.

ex Works. Also available as a two-seater, £360.
Pre-selector gearbox £25 extra.

The sports tourer on the M.G. Magnette chassis is outstandingly smart even in these days of attractive coachwork. The patent M.G. luggage carrier, similar to that on the Saloon, is employed, the same lavish dashboard equipment, and sensible side screens provide Saloon comfort when the hood is erected. The cut away doors and the flared scuttles give just that touch of smartness and practicability that is appreciated when the windscreen is folded flat and the speedometer needle soars up to eighty. As on all the other models, the upholstery is in real leather, the tyres " Fort Dunlop," and Triplex glass is a standard fitment.

REALLY FAST!
REALLY SAFE!

This 1934 PA-type Midget is painted in the distinctive brown-and-cream biscuit-like livery which characterized the three works-backed 'Cream Cracker' trailling team cars. The P-type superseded the J-type and used a new high-revving 847cc ohc engine. The front wings are braced to the radiator by tie-bars which carry the headlamps, minimizing the vibrations known as 'front-end dither'.

For 1934, the Magnette's wheelbase was standardized with the NA-series cars at 8ft (2,400mm), with the fuel tank now covered in. Its chassis was no longer of the simple ladder type and side-members were narrower at the front than the rear.

The specification of the new 1934 PA Midget included an 847cc three-bearing crankshaft ohc engine, four-speed gearbox and 12in brake drums. Both two- and four-seater versions were available in two-tone paintwork, with matching leather upholstery.

One of the most attractive closed models produced by MG – or indeed the industry in general – was the Airline Coupé of 1935, and it was certainly among Cecil Kimber's personal favourites. Its aerodynamics were understandably superior to the saloon and open-top models, and the wider doors provided easier access to the interior.

The Airline Coupé qualifies as one of the first grand touring cars. This one is built on a Magnette NA chassis, but it could also be based on the PA. Specialist coachbuilders active at the time included University Motors – also an MG main-dealer – Allinghams and Bertelli.

Based on the SA chassis, this 1938 drophead coupé was built by Salmons and Sons Ltd of Newport Pagnell along the lines patented by Tickfords, and has the look typical of late 1930s cabriolets. The car could be used with the hood in three positions: fully open; covering just the rear seats; or completely closed. Salmons also built a neat drophead body on the T-type Midget chassis.

The VA was made as a drophead coupé by Tickford in 1937 and further ventilation was provided by opening the pivoting windscreen. The four-seat tourer's specification, including 1,548cc engine and four-speed gearbox, was said by The Light Car *in 1937 to 'form a delightful compromise between the T-type Midget and 2.0-litre model'. Priced at £351, the VA's cost was increased by £5 if the 'Jackall' integral four-wheel jacking equipment was specified.*

The 1,292cc pushrod-engine TA of 1937, available only as a two-seater and capable of only 80mph (130km/h), was seen by dyed-in-the-wool MG enthusiasts as a regression. Its forté was reliability, however, and those campaigned in trials did well, although unlike many of its Midget predecessors, the TA was bought for touring rather than competition work.

For the 1939 TB engine, the stroke was shortened to give 1,250cc and the high-revving unit produced peak power at 5,252rpm. The crankshaft was counterbalanced accordingly and main bearings were of steel thin-wall type. Its production lifespan was brief, but examples are raced today in events like the VSCC Prescott Hillclimb.

Post-war austerity meant that sports-car production – and that of cars in general – was erratic, and MG was able to capitalize on this with the TC, which was ready to go in 1945. It was especially popular with American servicemen who remained in the UK after the war, and many TCs were shipped back home. This was the start of cult status for the marque in the USA. For eight years, until the advent of the Austin-Healey and Triumph TR2, the MGTC was the only mass-produced British sports car available – apart from the doubly expensive XK120.

The TD of 1950 was one of the least satisfactory MGs from the visual point of view, since it looked neither modern nor could it claim the rakish good looks of its predecessor: it looked staid by comparison. Nevertheless, during its three-year production run, it sold at a faster rate than any previous MG and was especially popular in the USA.

The TF was pretty enough, but was originally little more than a facelifted TD – brought in as a stop-gap when the proposals for the MGA foundered. The headlights were fared into the wings and the radiator grille slanted backwards, the overall effect being of a better proportioned, low-slung vehicle. The radiator cap was redundant, with the filler now under the bonnet. This item was a more conventional affair, with a push-button release and centre-hinged top, and the sides now had fixed valances.

In production from 1953 to 1958 as the ZA and later ZB model – seen here among 1958 café society – the Magnette was an excellent, well appointed sports saloon. The US Road and Track *magazine commented on the Magnette's 'surprisingly opulent interior', citing the wood-grain dash and leather-covered seating. They liked the driving position and found the interior comparatively spacious. Its ride quality was 'a little on the firm side', they said, 'but this no doubt contributes to better-than-average cornering characteristics'.*

What the sporting family motorist aspired to – other than a Mk VII Jaguar – in 1953: the Magnette ZA. With a pair of better-than-average front seats and a rear bench with fold-away central armrest, it could carry five people in relative comfort. Although the spare wheel was carried vertically in the left-hand side of the boot, there was still reasonable luggage space; access to the engine was also adequate, with the radiator grille incorporated in the rear-hinged bonnet.

MG's promotional material still majored on the 'Safety Fast' slogan, while continuing to hint at competition success. Introduced in 1955, four months after the company returned to racing with the three EX. 182 prototypes at Le Mans, the MGA was heralded by Autosport*'s John Bolster with the apt statement 'the racing car of today is the touring car of tomorrow!'*

The MGA roadster's chassis was a sturdy cross-braced box-section platform – almost a three-dimensional spaceframe – curving over the back axle and inwards towards the engine bay. The streamlined bodyshell was supported on the outer rails. In practical terms, the downside of the MGA's styling was the shallow boot, in which much of the space was taken up by the spare wheel. The chrome luggage racks – as fitted to this 1958 1500 – are an unavoidable blemish.

When the MG Midget appeared in 1961, it was greeted with headlines such as the 'Spritely Midget' beacuse of its shared styling and powertrain, and its modest 87.9mph (141.5km/h) top speed was forgiven by The Motor, *which said 'it's not what a car does, it's the way that it does it', referring to the light, sensitive steering and accurate control. Between 1961 and 1964, 16,080 Mk I Midgets were produced, compared with 20,450 virtually identical Mk II Sprites.*

Midget production lasted for nineteen years, although the original shape was much compromised with the fitment of impact bumpers in 1974. The classic shape is seen left, in the 1964 MkII model, with the somewhat less attractive Mk III G-AN5 type, produced from 1969 to 1974, to the right, wearing Rostyle wheels and rounded rear arches.

Demonstrating how life could be lived in the fast lane, this left-hooker appeared in the 1967 MGB GT catalogue. The model was launched late in 1965, and thoroughly justified its gran turismo *label: it was a reasonably fast, well-mannered sports coupé with enough luggage space for two to go touring in comfort. Access through the large top-hinged rear door was excellent and the small rear bench seat could even accommodate a small child or two.*

The MGB GT V8 was a little late on the scene. By August 1973 when BL launched it – in coupé form only – erstwhile Mini dicer Ken Costello had been shoe-horning Rover V8s into MGBs for three years and Morgan's Plus 8 was already five years old. Indeed, Abingdon engineers had long ago tried the Daimler SP250 V8 in the MGB. Whatever, fewer engineering changes were necessary to install the all-alloy 3,528cc Rover V8 in the tried and trusted shell than implanting the earlier straight-six in the MGC, but stifling emissions regulations meant the de-tuned 137bhp Range Rover unit was fitted. This chrome-bumper model is equipped with a retro-fit front air dam, ostensibly to improve aerodynamics, if not aesthetics.

In May 1982, BL applied the MG badge to the Metro hatchback, equipping it with the single carburettor 1,275cc engine and more refined interior. In October 1982 the MG Metro Turbo was introduced, giving a top speed of 112mph and 0–60mph time of 9.9 seconds. The MG Metro was built at Longbridge adjacent to the old Mini plant and trimmed on the same line as the Mini.

After twenty-five years, the BMC works' competitions department at Abingdon was closed down in 1980. But in 1982, Austin Rover got Williams Grand Prix Engineering to build a prototype for the four-wheel drive Metro 6R4 project, pitching into world-class rallying against the might of the Group B monsters, including Lancia's Delta S4 and Ford's RS200. Effectively silhoutte racing cars, their specifications took advantage of extremely liberal regulations. David Llewellin made the mud fly on the 1986 Lombard RAC Rally, but 6R4's shovel-like front spoiler also made water-splashes hazardous. Llewellin was one of seven top names driving Metro 6R4s on the 1986 UK event. Despite being plagued by differential failures due to increased output from their twin-turbo V6 engines, the cars filled four places on the results sheet, from Pond/Arthur in sixth to Llewellin/Short in ninth position.

The first all-new MG to be produced in its own right in thirty-two years, the MGF was launched at the Geneva Show in March 1995. Intended as a rival to the likes of the Mazda MX-5 and Honda CRX, the all-steel bodied MGF is only available from 150 out of 660 potential Rover dealerships. Two versions are available, both powered by the 1.8-litre K-series twin-cam – also found in the Morgan Plus 4. The top-of-the-range MGF, with variable valve timing, is good for 130mph and makes the 0-60mph dash in under 7 seconds. Much of the componentry is sourced from the extensive Rover Group parts bins, including the Metro front subframe and switchgear.

MG N-Type Magnette

The final incarnation of the small six-cylinder MG was the N-type, introduced in March 1934, which effectively replaced the Magna and K-series Magnette. It had a new chassis and its 1,271cc KD engine was tuned to produce 54bhp. Six racing variants known as NEs were built and were successful in the 1934 Tourist Trophy even without superchargers. Here a pair of NE Magnettes brave the elements on Douglas sea front in 1937.

A Magnette NA draws a crowd during a trial on the Nailsworth Ladder, Somerset. At left behind a Singer Sports Nine are Cecil Kimber, his wife Rene and one of their two daughters, who seem unconcerned by the activity.

Three of the racing NEs formed a team known as the Three Musketeers and excelled in trialling in the mid 1930s. Here is Musketeer 'Aramis' on the Devon trial in 1935.

Evidence of the Three Musketeers' success can be seen here in the spoils of victory displayed by one of the team members. In 1938 the Musketeers eventually fitted supercharged TA engines in their red-painted cars.

The first of three N-type Magnettes gets away on a stage of the West Hants Car Club Relay trial.

An NA Magnette is reduced to two horsepower on a hilly trial section. The sign warning enthusiasts of the dangers of spectating on the bend is thus somewhat redundant.

5

Major A.T.G. 'Goldie' Gardner is pushed out onto the Brooklands circuit in his K.3 Magnette in 1936. This is the ex-Ron Horton car, which had set a new lap record of 115.55mph (186.04km/h) on the outer circuit three years previously.

Goldie Gardner poses in his special-bodied single seater K.3 Magnette on the Brooklands banking, the scene of the car's earlier triumphs in the hands of Ron Horton.

MG T-Type

Underpinnings of the MG TA-type Midget; chassis dimensions were increased by 3ft 9in (1,143mm) to 7ft 10in (2,388mm) – almost identical to those of the Q-type. The TA was not available without bodywork however.

With the take-over of MG by Morris Motors, there was considerable anxiety about the prospects for future models. With the abandonment of the small ohc engines in favour of Wolseley 10/40-derived 1,292cc pushrod ohv units, the concern seemed justified. In practice, however, the TA was able to out-perform the old PB, and this couple with their 1938 Coupé model perhaps typify a more relaxed type of owner than the hard-bitten sporting enthusiast of earlier days.

Bearing in mind the attitude of the Morris hierarchy to sports cars, it was no mean feat that Cecil Kimber managed to maintain Midget production at all, let alone retain the marque's individuality. In fact the TA heralded a new and more sophisticated MG Midget, with advantages such as the Tickford Coupé's folding rear header. The TA's larger two-seater body gave it virtually the same size cockpit as the Magnette.

Specification of the TA was rather better than the PB and included a synchromesh gearbox and Lockheed hydraulic brakes. Over 3,000 TAs were produced between 1936 and 1939 and, like this hill climber, many were used in competition.

The TA of G.E. Ansell is about to be given the all clear for his run in the 1936 Poole Speed Trials.

An MG TA passes a stricken 1923 Aston Martin on a woodland trial section. The driver appears to be taking a wider line than previous competitors, to the obvious apprehension of his passenger.

Autocar magazine reported on 18 September 1936 that the TA seemed oddly to lack 'the familiar exhaust burble' of the ohc engines, but hinted that the TA exhaust system would be adjusted to 'restore more of an MG note'. Perhaps that is what the spectators on this MCC London–Land's End trial are listening so intently for.

A.W. Turnbull runs out of road in his Midget TA on the London–Edinburgh trial. The crew of the Jaguar SS100 in the background have presumably already retired.

MGs enjoyed an excellent reputation on the continent and nowhere more so than in Germany. This modified MG TA is pictured in the paddock at the Nurburgring in 1938. It looks incongruous in the national silver racing colour, and the swastika emblem is a reminder of the regime which funded Germany's dominant racing programme.

The TB Midget was introduced in April 1939 and, because of the outbreak of war, only 379 units were produced. It was externally identical to the TA apart from the creased rear wings, which would reappear on the TC.

The TB's centre-hinged bonnet is raised to reveal the short-stroke, larger bore 1,250cc XPAG engine, a modified version of the new Morris Ten unit, which proved more robust than the earlier TA motor. This unit continued to be used to power MGs until 1953. It was more amenable to tuning, more free-revving and enabled a lower rear axle ratio to be used.

Cockpit of the TB Midget, with leather-covered dash, prominent spangled plastic four-spoke steering wheel, and rev-counter directly ahead of the driver and speedo in front of the passenger. This layout remained essentially unchanged with the TC.

MG's SA, VA and WA Saloons

The corporate restructuring of William Morris's Nuffield Organization and the reorganization of MG led to a revival of the big 18/80 sized car, and the six-cylinder SA four-door saloon was introduced in 1935. By the time production commenced, engine capacity was raised to 2,288cc. This model is on the promenade at Brighton for the 1952 Daily Express *Rally.*

Shortly after the SA saloon came out, an elegant drop-head coupé designed and built by Salmons was introduced. Despite the cabriolet top, there was still a tendency for the passenger compartment to overheat.

Challenging terrain for an SA 2.3-litre drop-head coupé and a P-type Midget, pictured in May 1939. The SA models suffered from delays in production because of the desire to standardize components within the company – foreshadowing BMC – and many sales were lost to Jaguar as customers were enticed away by the new SS saloon. Morris Motors had seriously underestimated the appeal and efficient production of the William Lyons creation.

The SA may not have been a sports car as such, rather a reasonably fast, reliable touring car. It was sufficiently competent for racing star and journalist T.H. 'Tommy' Wisdom to drive one in the 1937 Mille Miglia. This 1937 2.0-litre Charlesworth-bodied four-door roadster is competing on the 1938 Scottish Rally.

Bodywork for the VA tourer was made by Morris Bodies rather than Charlesworth. This example, wearing Ace wheel-discs, passes the judges' bench on the 1939 RAC Brighton Rally.

The SA was followed by the VA, using scaled-down but otherwise similar body styling, and powered by the ohv 1,548cc four-cylinder engine. This shooting brake with its headlights shrouded for wartime, is an unusual model for an MG, although 'woodies' in general were popular estate cars at the time.

The driver of this two-door 1.5-litre SA tourer appears to be assessing traction potential during the 1939 MCC Land's End trial. The lowered windscreen helps reduce wind resistance, making an 80mph (130km/h) top speed attainable.

The VA model had the spare wheel mounted on the nearside running-board. Cecil Kimber considered the VA to be one of his best designs, aesthetically, and his own saloon version was fitted with a tuned 1,703cc engine – it was also regular Abingdon practice to give press demonstrators similar treatment.

The WA of 1938 used the large SA body, with longer bonnet and wider rear track, plus a re-vamped interior giving better ergonomics. It was powered by a 2.6-litre six-cylinder engine unique in the Nuffield group at the time.

The four-seater drophead coupé version of the WA was a handsome car indeed, but few were produced because bodybuilders Charlesworth had given up producing automobile coachwork by the Spring of 1939. Notable customers for this model were Goldie Gardner and the Glasgow Constabulary.

Spectators line the promenade to watch a competitor in the 1952 Brighton Rally swing his 1937 VA tourer between the straw bales in the driving test section.

This rather unlikely looking vehicle was the MG SA which Tommy Wisdom drove in the 1937 Mille Miglia. However, his race ended with an accident on a wet road near Florence, and the car was subsequently rebuilt by the factory and used as a works' service pick-up. It appears here in wartime guise.

Record Breaking

Record breaking was a much more widespread and intense activity in pre-war years and although MG had officially withdrawn from competition, Cecil Kimber prevailed upon the management for works backing to pursue speed records. This is Goldie Gardner's EX.135 at Brooklands in 1938.

The wooden mock-up which will determine the shape of EX.135's streamlined all-enveloping bodywork. This would be designed by Reid Railton, who went on to style John Cobb's record breaker, and made by Jaray.

EX.135 was built up using chassis components from George Eyston's Magic Magnette and the ex-Ron Horton K.3 Magnette – already raced in more conventional form by Gardner. The rolling chassis of EX.135 is exposed to reveal the 1,086cc K.3 engine with its square-section exhaust manifold, scuttle spaceframe and massive Zoller supercharger behind the radiator. Tyres are virtually slicks.

The cockpit of EX.135, revealing the recumbent driving position, ovoid aircraft-style steering wheel, four-speed shift and a comprehensive array of instruments including supercharger rpm, boost gauge, tachometer and speedo.

Having taken the 1,100cc record up to 203.2mph (327km/h) on the autobahn at Dessau in 1939, Major Goldie Gardner took EX.135 to Italy in 1946 to run in 750cc form on the autostrada. Accompanied by a cloud of steam, mechanics wheel the machine out for its west-to-east run on the first day, 27 July. It clocked 145mph (233km/h) over one kilometre, and over 150mph (240km/h) the following day.

The car ran with a variety of engines, including a six-cylinder unit, pictured here on the test bench in June 1946, with team members in attendance including Gardner, centre, and Chas Shorrock at right.

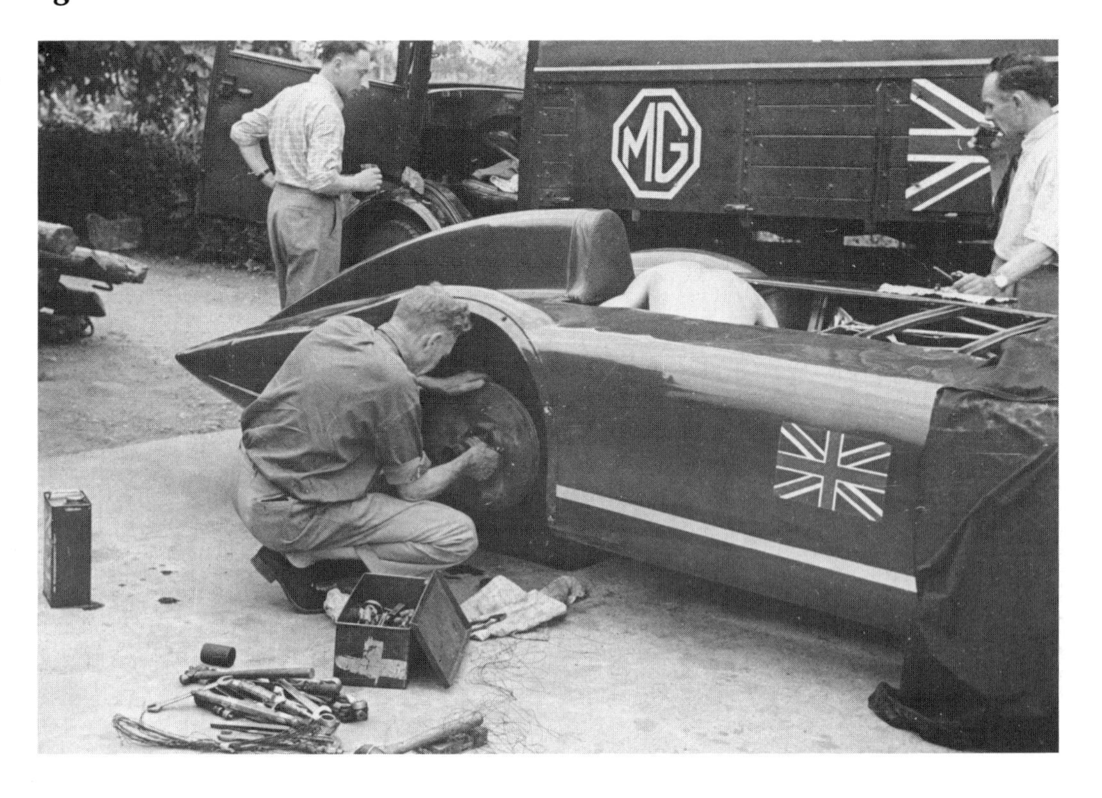

Technician L.G. Kesleton changes a brake disc on EX.135, while Kenneth Baines, left, and Chas Shorrock enjoy a glass of Chianti.

Goldie Gardner poses in EX.135 for the media, with technician L.G. Kesleton, left, and a proprietorial Chas Shorrock, right, surrounded by the tifosi, *who look merely curious.*

The whole team behind Gardner's Italian record-breaking venture, pictured on the Brescia–Bergamo autostrada; from the left are Alec Baines, Syd Enever, Goldie Gardner, Reg 'Jacko' Jackson, Chas Shorrock, Kenneth Baines, and L.G. Kesleton. The Topolino behind provides a counterpoint to EX.135.

Major Gardner is briefed by a technician, while team members Shorrock and Kesleton look anxious as EX.135 is fuelled up for a run.

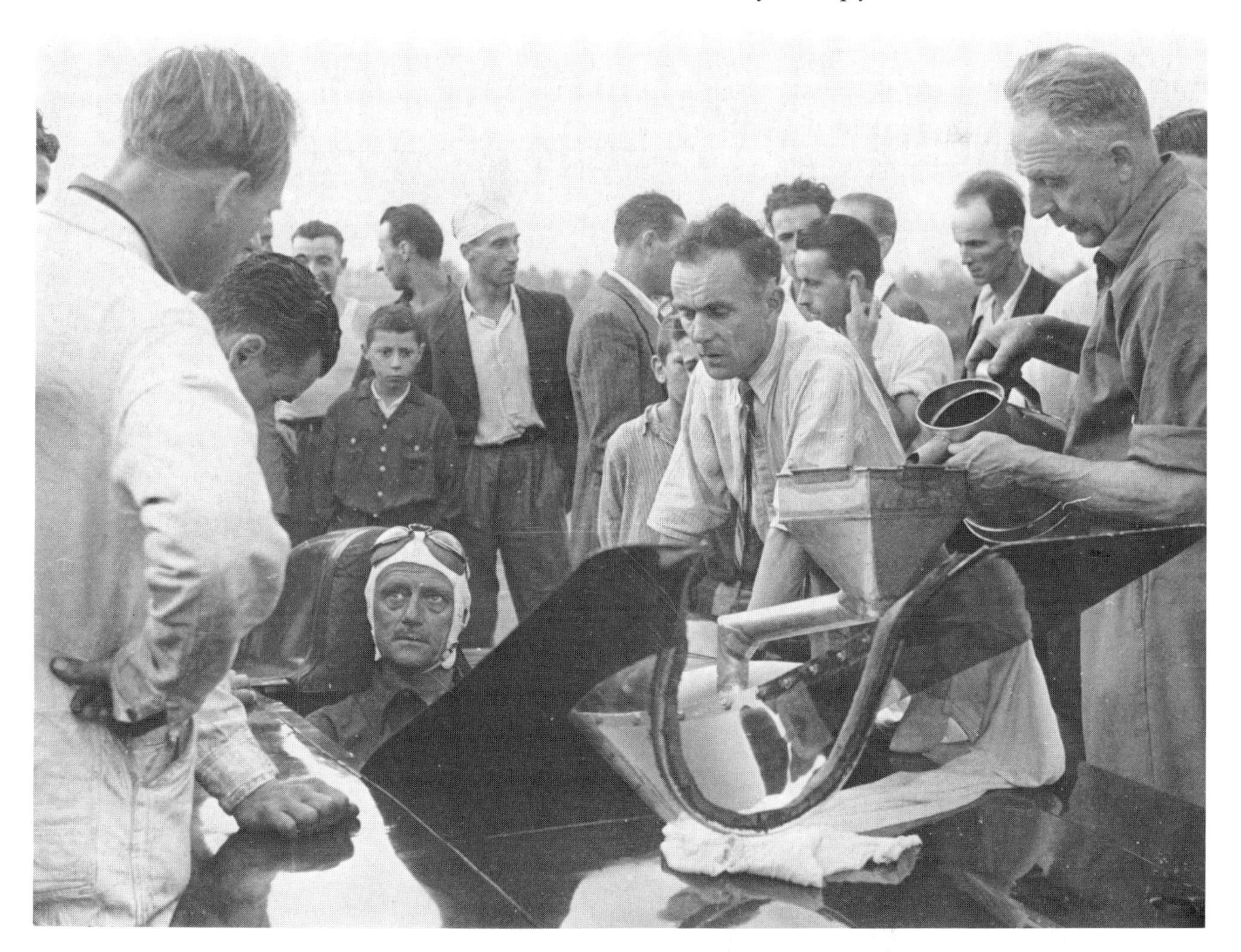

Goldie Gardner set a whole host of records in classes up to 2.0 litres in EX.135, including a five mile run at the Bonneville Salt flats, Utah, USA, in 1952. Using the 1,250cc Midget engine, he achieved 189.5mph (305km/h). The car is clearly running a six-cylinder motor in the picture, and the exhaust pipes have been blocked off to keep the dirt out.

EX.135 was even tried out with a six-cylinder Jaguar XK-type twin-cam engine.

Goldie Gardner's feats are chronicled beside EX.135, on display in 1947. The car can be seen today in the British Motor Heritage Collection at Gaydon.

MG Post-War: the TC

The Kent Constabulary takes delivery of seven MG TC Midgets in 1946. Introduced in October 1945, the TC was essentially the same as the TB, but the body was now 4in (102mm) wider. The future Duke of Edinburgh was an early customer.

An MG TC cornered hard at Silverstone's Beckett's corner in 1948. Headlights are reversed for improved aerodynamics.

The standard TC cost £527 in 1946, but this TC's owner has lavished on it a variety of extras including air horns, spotlights, wing mirrors, wind deflectors, luggage rack and a winged radiator cap.

This is the TC rolling chassis, produced between 1945 and 1949, and fitted with the ohv 1,250cc XPAG pushrod engine, half-elliptic leaf springs and drum brakes all round. Springs were now shackle-mounted instead of in sliding trunnions.

Rear three-quarter shot shows off the TC's rakish lines and four-piece weather equipment to good effect, particularly the twin rear windows. Considering this is a publicity photo, there is an interesting mix of tyres: the spare is virtually bald and the rear has a chunkier pattern than the front one. A sign of post-war austerity perhaps.

MG Y-Type Saloons

The MG YA was launched in April 1947, based on the new Morris Eight chassis which used rack-and-pinion steering and an independent wishbone and coil spring front suspension set up designed by Alec Issigonis. The car gained a reputation for good ride, and its 1,250cc XPAG engine could be tuned to provide the sort of performance which enabled Gardner to take Dick Benn's car (seen here outside Brittan's Garage, Brighton) to 104mph (167km/h) in 1948.

Post-war steel supplies were strictly limited, with exporters getting priority, and thus many YAs were sold in foreign markets. The YT touring bodied version was particularly popular in Australia, although it was never as successful as the TC.

The Y-type's rather dumpy saloon body, with B-post door hinges, was based on that of the Series E Morris Eight, and its launch had been planned for 1941. Its styling was given the MG look by Gerald Palmer. This is the 1952 YB, which had a hypoid rear axle and smaller wheels.

The three-car MG team pictured during the 1953 Daily Express *RAC Rally, with Len Shaw, (left), Reg Holt, Stan Astbury, Freddie Finnemore and Geoff Holt, with their Y-type saloons.*

An MG YA is flagged off from the Arc de Triomphe checkpoint on the 1954 Monte Carlo Rally. The gendarmes must have been puzzled by the leek attached to the radiator grille.

A Y-type is prepared in the paddock at Silverstone at a club meeting in 1956. The pits have changed somewhat since then.

MG Specials

Some specials had a lengthy career: built in 1951, this Lester MG is in action at Oulton Park in 1957. There is a hint of Alta and Cooper Bristol about the frontal styling.

The 1950s saw a number of MG specials in action. Here, Bill Coleman's 'Jaguette' – an N-type Magnette chassis fitted with a 1939 2.5-litre Jaguar engine and Morris Eight grille – takes part in the 1952 Brighton speed trials.

R.W. 'Dick' Jacobs' 1950 MG TD Special may have been influenced by Frazer-Nash or Healey Silverstone styling. Five years on, driving one of the three works MGAs, Jacobs was severely injured in a crash at the ill-starred 1955 Le Mans 24-Hours, although his team-mates managed fifth and sixth in class. Jacobs later ran teams of Magnettes, MGAs and Midgets with much success.

The mechanicals and running gear of a pre-war MG such as a PB Midget would have been very attractive as a means of building a Clubmans' special in post-war years.

By the mid 1950s, a new industry had sprung up producing a wide range of fibreglass bodies; Dick Jacobs' other TD Special is clad in an RGS Atalanta coupé body – as used by TVR at the same time. Also seen in the Goodwood paddock on 7 June 1954 are a Lotus Mk 6 and the Lester MG.

This sports racer, driven by Chris Lawrence at the BARC Goodwood meeting on 22 September 1956, is actually one of the 1935 Musketeer Magnettes, using an all-enveloping body style rather similar to a contemporary Connaught or Lister.

MG TD

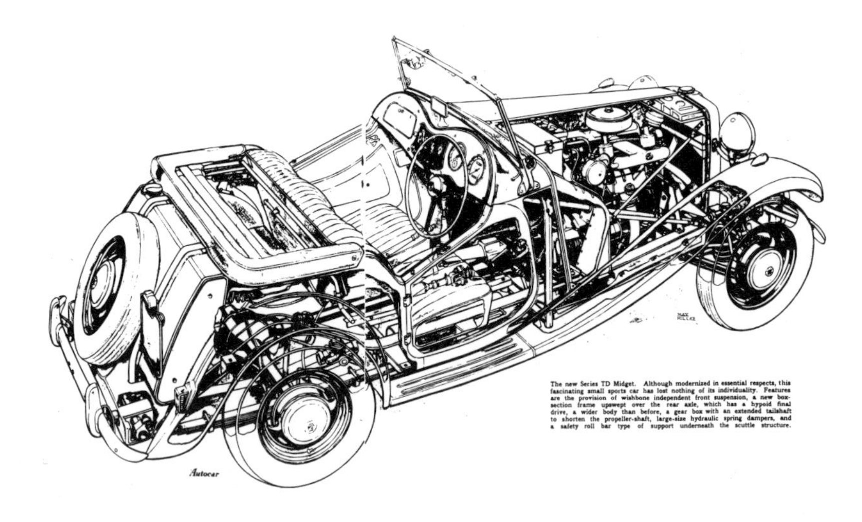

The TD seen in cross-section in this Max Millar drawing for Autocar *magazine was an advance on the TC theme by virtue of its wishbone front suspension, hypoid final drive and extended tailshaft on the gearbox to shorten the propshaft. Hydraulic dampers and an anti-roll bar were fitted.*

Although the lines of the TD – 4in (102mm) wider than the TC – were sufficiently popular with enthusiasts for some 10,000 units to be sold in 1950, it was showing its age by 1953 when production ended – 29,664 units were produced in total. This left-hooker is starting a timed run on a 1952 trial.

On his way to Breakfast at Tiffany's, *a youthful George Peppard is in the driving seat of this 1950 model – complete with period white-wall tyres. Perhaps an MGA would have been more appropriate for the future* A-Team *leader.*

A 1951 TD, complete with hand-operated spotlight, waiting for the off during the 1953 Daily Express *National Motor Museum Rally and Concours d' Elegance*

Pictured on the 1952 Circuit of Ireland rally, the curvaceous dashboard of J.G. Allen's MG TD shows the speedometer now alongside the rev-counter. A pair of goggles is at the ready in the glove locker, along with a pair of stop watches and a pair of corduroy trousers in the driving seat.

Sporting sunglasses to counter the wintry sunshine, D.G. Johnston sets out on 'Paddy's Brae' during the Ulster Automobile Club's 1953 Boxing Day Trial. His passenger bounces up and down in the TD to increase traction in the mud.

MG TF

The T-type MG in its final and most elegant incarnation, the TF, launched at the Earls Court Show in October 1953. The centrally grouped instrumentation was set in a sloping fascia, and featured dials with octagonal faces, and the wiper motor was concealed under the scuttle. Originally powered by the 1,250cc TD engine, the Mark II of 1954 used the 1,466cc XPEG unit.

In 1953 Autosport *commented that the TF was built 'for the non-competition-minded class of purchaser' and that it retained 'the familiar Midget lines evolved long ago in 1933 with the J2'. The 1.5-litre engine was initially in such short supply that the TF was launched with the Mk II TD's 1,250cc unit, receiving the Magnette motor in 1955 – of which the American Road and Track commented: 'Too little, too late, so what'. In 1954, the magazine still regarded it as 'America's best sports car buy'.*

Magnette ZA

The merger of the Nuffield Organization and Austin Motor Company in 1952 led to a rationalization of models within the newly-formed British Motor Corporation. Consequently the MG Magnette ZA of 1953 shared its Gerald Palmer-designed Italianate (see Pinin Farina's 1948 Lancia Aprilia cabriolet, etc.) body styling with the Wolseley 4/44 and was powered by BMC's 1,489cc B-series engine. Along with its Wolseley and Riley siblings, the Abingdon-built Magnette was an early example of unit-construction – no ladder chassis, but a light, mass-produced bodyshell. ZA production totalled 18,076 units.

MG aficionados were incensed that the much revered Magnette name should be applied to a saloon model, but the cars were aired in competition from time to time. This 1955 Monte Carlo Rally entrant has inadvertently customized the front of his ZA on the Col Bayard.

The semi-works aluminium-panelled ZA Magnette of Gregor Grant/Sammy Davis at the Paris checkpoint on the 1956 Monte Carlo Rally.

Bonneville Salt Flats: Back in the USA

The next MG record breaker was EX.179, built under Syd Enever's direction at Abingdon in 1954, and driven by George Eyston and American racing driver Ken Miles. The cockpit was over to the left of the chassis, instead of EX.135's central position, and it was powered by an unsupercharged 1,466cc TF-derived engine.

Ken Miles (pictured here) and Captain George Eyston set no fewer than thirty-five time and distance records at Utah during August 1954. Fastest run achieved 154 mph and the car ran for 12 hours at 120mph (195km/h).

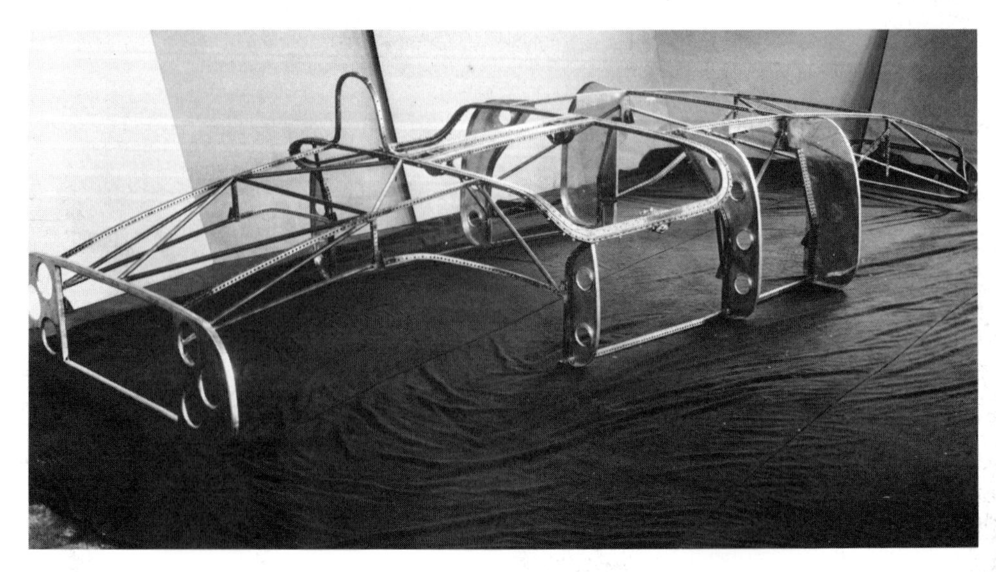

The elegant space-frame constructed to support the bodywork of Ex.179 was attached to a far beefier box-section chassis. The complete car can be seen at the British Motor Industry Heritage collection at Gaydon.

The chassis of EX.179 was originally one of two intended for a prototype MGA, and the body was in aluminium. Suspension was basically standard TF issue, but the front dampers were augmented by Andrex friction-type units and dual units were fitted at the rear. Brakes were Lockheed drums and the pressed-steel wheels were shod with Dunlop racing tyres. In this picture, the 30-gallon (136-litre) fuel tank has yet to be fitted.

Ken Miles and John Lockett congratulate one another after taking the World Class F record to 170mph (274km/h) and running for twelve hours at nearly 142mph (229km/h) in 1956. For this visit to Bonneville's weird landscape, EX.179 was in right-hand drive and fitted with a supercharged MGA twin-cam engine, at that time in the experimental stage.

For the 1957 programme, BMC had upped its profile and improved the livery of EX.179's bodywork. David Ash, seen here, was one of three works drivers – Tommy Wisdom and Phil Hill were the others – to raise the class record to 143.47mph (230.99km/h).

MGA

As far back as 1951, MG development engineer Syd Enever and general manager John Thornley had planned a new sports car with a streamlined body to replace the TD. The project was vetoed by Sir Leonard Lord who preferred not to jeopardize sales of the new Austin-Healey, but it finally came to fruition in 1955 when three MGA prototypes were raced at Le Mans under the code-name EX.182. Ken Wharton tries one at Silverstone prior to the Le Mans event.

The MGA was launched in September 1955 and brought the company right up-to-date stylistically. It was powered by the 1,489cc four-cylinder B-series engine, tuned up to yield 72bhp. Door handles were absent in early models, and access was gained through the side screen if the hood was erected. Steel wheels were standard issue, but wires were optional.

An MGA 1500 with fly-screen gets a run at Silverstone, 25 August 1956. The driver models the archetypal bone-dome.

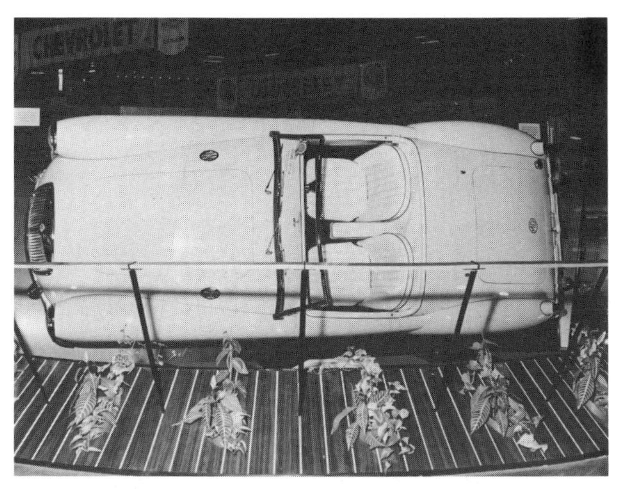

This spectacular 1956 Motor Show setting gave the crowds a dramatic view of the MGA 1500 – as if viewed from above or high up on the banking.

An MGA gets an uplifting experience in this Nuffield Organization publicity photo of the new detachable hard-top, released on 12 October 1956.

Left-hand drive and white-wall tyres indicate clearly the market MG was aiming at – and indeed, doing very nicely in. This is the 1600 model, running a 1,588cc straight-four B-series engine introduced in 1959.

From October 1957 the MGA was available as a coupé. The well-proportioned pressed steel top was welded to the body and complemented by its wrap-around rear window. Door windows could be wound up and down. It was still only a two-seater, but it provided a calmer environment for the touring motorist.

ZB Magnette

An indication of the changing times was the penchant for two-tone colour schemes in the late 1950s. The ZB 'Varitone' Magnette of 1956 came in several different combinations, and the car's curvaceous lines benefited from a larger rear window. Total production of ZBs was 18,574.

The specification of the ZB Magnette included improved suspension, a slight increase in power – to 68bhp – and some cars were fitted with the 'Manumatic' clutchless semi-automatic transmission system. The car's improved handling is demonstrated at Druid's Bend, Brands Hatch, on 10 May 1959.

Bonneville Again

Extensive wind tunnel testing showed that a teardrop shape produced the most promising aerodynamic configuration and EX.181 was the culmination of MG's record breaking cars. Here Stirling Moss gets a taste of 'the real thing' at Bonneville in 1957.

The mid-engined chassis of EX.181 matched its teardrop body with a narrower track at the rear than the front. The cockpit was in the nose and the tail tapered away at the rear – sometimes with fin, sometimes without. MG personnel including Chas Shorrock survey its presentation, while at the rear lurks EX.179, by now running as a test-bed for the impending Sprite – produced at Abingdon from 1959.

Stirling Moss sits in the diminutive cockpit, accompanied by MG general manager and Car Club co-founder John Thornley (left), and chassis designer Syd Enever. Today, EX.181 is among twenty-five or so classic MGs on display at Gaydon.

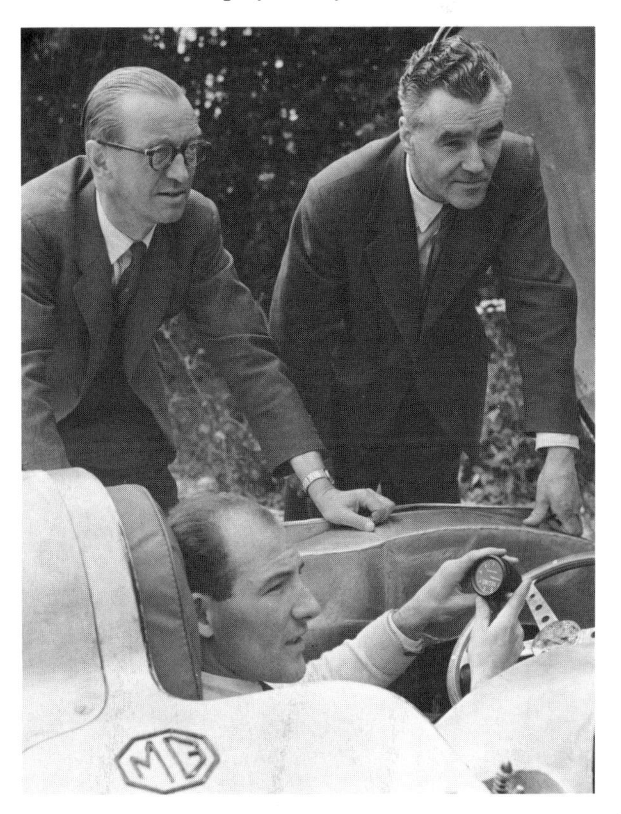

The experimental supercharged 1,489cc MG twin-cam engine which powered EX.181 on its record-breaking venture in 1957. The supercharger and SU carburettors are mounted in a compact arrangement to the lower left-hand side to clear the bodywork. In 1959 it was bored out to 1,506cc for Phil Hill to attack the 2.0-litre class records, which he left at 254.9mph (410.4km/h) – the fastest speed ever achieved by an MG.

Cockpit of EX.181, in which a recumbent Stirling Moss reached 245.6mph (395.4km/h) at Bonneville in 1957. Steering columns have seldom been so short and the wheel's position is positively bus-like. Instrumentation – comprising water temperature, tachometer, fuel pressure – appears an afterthought. Moss was clearly undeterred by the prospect of only a single disc brake to check his speed.

MGA Post 1960

This 1958 MGA front hub assembly features Dunlop-made disc brake, and in 1959 the 1600 model was fitted with Lockheed products. The Twin-Cam had discs all round, as did the 1600 De Luxe, built in Mk I and Mk II form between 1960 and 1962; this model was said to have been introduced to 'use up' all the specialized components left over when Twin-Cam production ended in 1960.

Another MG with a titled owner was this 1600 MGA Coupé twin-cam, belonging to HRH Prince Michael of Kent and pictured at Hohe barracks, West Germany in May 1963.

The MGA Coupé body was more aerodynamic than the roadster and thus a better option as a competition model. This one is running in a 1959 BARC meeting at Goodwood, dampened by an April shower.

This styling exercise, known as EX.214, was based on Abingdon sketches and built on a Mk II 1600 chassis by Pietro Frua's Piedmont design house in Italy. The grille is redolent of the Pinin Farina Magnette, but the overall design bears strong similarities to other contemporary Frua work, such as the Maserati 3500GT.

MG Magnette Mk III and Mk IV

This is a Nuffield Organization press photo of the MG badged version of BMC's Pinin Farina-styled family saloon. The only components which linked this model to the ZA and ZB Magnette which preceded it were the drivetrain: engine, gearbox and rear axle. It was built at Cowley from 1959 to 1961 along with its four virtually identical siblings.

The Mk IV Magnette had a slightly longer wheelbase and wider track than the Mk III, with anti-roll bars front and rear, and its handling was thus much improved. Performance was also better as the engine capacity was increased to 1,622cc, but the body shape was still fundamentally the same and it staggered on largely unloved until 1968.

MGA in Competition

A dice at Woodcote corner on Silverstone's Club circuit during the 1961 Birkett Six-Hour Relay, with R. Ide's MGA 1600 neck and neck with Patrick McNally's Morgan Plus 4.

Bob Olthoff's MGA Twin-Cam in full cry at Silverstone's Copse Corner during the 750 MC Six-Hour Relay, August 1961. The event was won by Sebring Sprites, and Olthoff was forced to retire in the first hour when his floorboards caught fire. The South African registration number seen here was later replaced with UK plate YRX 310.

An MGA Twin-Cam Coupé broadsides out of Woodcote corner during a club meeting. The white-wall tyres are an affectation on the race circuit, but one Twin-Cam feature evident here is the centre-lock steel wheels. Fast for its day, this model was perhaps too potent for its own good. It acquired a reputation for drinking oil, needing constant fettling, access was difficult and widespread service back-up was unavailable in the USA. It was taken out of production in 1960 with only 2,111 units built.

J.H. Carter tries hard at Silverstone as he aims his 1500 MGA around Copse, while keeping ahead of a Coupé during a September club meeting.

Its bumpers removed to reduce weight, the MGA of P.J. McCallum crests Druids' Hill and swings into the Druids' hairpin at Brands Hatch, 24 September 1961

MGA 1500 roadsters go down the line to the final inspection area at Abingdon. The engine was enlarged from 1,489cc to 1,588cc in 1959 and although the Twin-Cam model shared the same block, no other BMC vehicle powered by the pushrod B-series engine ever used this capacity.

In 1962, MGA production reached the 100,000 mark, commemorated on the number plate of this 1600 Mk II. The facelifted model was distinguished from its predecessor by the more vertically-set grille bars and horizontal tail-light clusters.

Return of the Midget

When the Abingdon-built Sprite was rebodied in July 1961 – frontal treatment by Donald Healey, rear end by Syd Enever – a badge-engineered MG version was introduced at the same time, featuring a full-width grille and slightly more upmarket trim package. The two models shared the same running gear, with the MG proving more popular in the market-place than its more austere rival.

What appears pretty basic today was considered perfectly adequate cockpit trim in 1961 and suited the Midget's young enthusiasts. The plastic steering wheel was on the large side, but the car could be rowed along rapidly enough by deft use of the four-speed gear shift.

The A-series ohv straight-four, fed by a pair of SU carburettors, is a neat fit under the Midget's rear-hinged bonnet. Compression ratio is 9:1, and the 948cc engine delivers 46bhp at 5,500rpm.

By March 1964, the Midget had grown up a bit and the Mk II dash was more styled with less haphazard placement of controls. The rear-view mirror could now be moved vertically up and down on a central bar.

The Mk III Midget was introduced in 1966 and was powered by the 65bhp 1,275cc engine. The lower-profile hood was now of the fold-away variety and this was effectively the last Midget before British Leyland's more swingeing changes reduced the model's aesthetic appeal.

Like the Mk II Midget, the Mk III model had wind-up windows and was basically unchanged internally. The fold-away hood was covered by a neat tonneau and the shelf behind the seats could accommodate a small amount of luggage – or as was sometimes the case, a recumbent person.

The Series 1 Land Rovers in the background would probably be better placed on this terrain than the Mk I Midget, roughing it on a club trial. A child is being carried as ballast.

Autocross emerged as a serious form of motor sport in the mid 1960s and attracted a host of seemingly unsuitable vehicles. At any rate, the Spridget was a more nimble car than the Spitfire.

Abingdon's export drive: a variety of Austin-Healeys, Mk I Midgets and Mk II Sprites – with sliding windows – plus sundry Alpines and tractors, awaits shipment to the New World from Cardiff docks.

MG 1100 and 1300

The MG 1100 – here in Mk II guise with cut-back tail fins – was BMC's top-of-the-range 1100 model. It shared the same bodyshell and hydrolastic suspension system as its Austin, Morris, Riley, Wolseley and Vanden Plas stable-mates, but its twin SUs gave a slightly better performance. The MG 1100 did have a competition career of sorts, works cars being rallied in 1962 by David Siegle-Morris/Rupert Jones and in 1963 by Pauline Mayman/Val Domleo, and Raymond Baxter/Ernie McMillen.

A two-door version of the Pininfarina-styled MG 1100, in US trim. BMC had high hopes for sales in the States, where the MG badge held much kudos. In all, 124,860 MG 1100s were built between 1962 and 1967, and 32,549 units of the MG 1300 version were produced from 1967 to 1973.

Thanks to the transverse engine mounting, the MG 1100 provided passengers with a relatively spacious interior and despite its sometimes derided badge-engineering image, the concept of the car was excellent. The original MG 1100 engine was good for 55bhp, but mercifully the MG 1300 Mk II had a higher compression ratio and stronger crankshaft, lifting it to 70bhp and the potential of 97mph (156km/h) top speed.

The wood-grain veneer dash of the Mk II MG 1100 displays a restrained austerity for 1967, although the speedo is only just fashionable.

By the time the model was nearing the end of its production life, it had become the MG 1300 Mk II, having gained the 1,275cc engine in 1967. Apart from improved performance and better specification, the dash now took on a more realistic sporting aspect, although the wheel is still at a Mini-esque angle.

Before John Cooper's 'hot' Minis were accepted by BMC as the way forward, this prototype MG cabriolet was commissioned from Pininfarina. Its sister car also never progressed beyond prototype stage. Code-named ADO 35, it was a coupé with a Magnette grille and Cooper S running gear, and is currently owned by MG buff Richard Howard.

MGB

One of the best-liked sports cars in the world, the MGB was launched in October 1962. This Nuffield Organization press picture shows the MGB in US trim, with whitewall tyres, left-hand drive and Stateside licence-plate holder.

The concept of the MGB GT is clearly evident in this 1959 prototype, EX.205/1, and one of the contemporary fibreglass specialists, Ashley, produced a hard top for the MGB which was an even closer copy. EX.205/1 lacked a hatch-back, however, and bore more similarity to the MGA from the front, since it was intended as a unit-construction successor to the A.

Expectations were high for the MGB, which used many modified components from the MGA. A product of the fertile minds of Enever and Thornley, it was of monocoque body-chassis construction and was actually heavier than the MGA because of the extra steel required to provide structural rigidity. Nevertheless it was a huge aesthetic success.

The early MGB cockpit was certainly roomy enough for tall drivers, and there was a certain logic about the placement of instruments and switches, even if the presentation was not so attractive. The overdrive switch – if one was fitted – lay ahead and just to the right of the steering wheel and effectively provided another two gear ratios.

The B-series engine was the cast-iron head and block straight-four ohv unit, displacing 1,798cc. It produced 95bhp at 5,400rpm and until September 1964 there was a three-bearing crankshaft, and five thereafter, which meant it matched the new Austin 1800 block.

Old versus new at this Silverstone club meeting. The MGB takes the chequered flag ahead of the MGA, but it has evidently been a close-run race. Clearly one competitor was not so tenacious. The MGB's forte was its stamina and reliability, demonstrated by Andrew Hedges/Julian Vernaeve at the Nürburgring in 1966, where they won the 84-hour Marathon de la Route outright against the strongest opposition.

In the right hands – Roger Enever (son of Syd), and Bill Nicholson to name but two leading protagonists – the MGB could excel in major events; John Rhodes/Warwick Banks even won the 1965 Guards 1000 international sports car race outright. This dramatic Silverstone pit stop, also in 1965, shows the car of brother and sister Trevor and Anita Taylor, wearing several competition accoutrements, including Perspex headlight fairings and bonnet strap.

The MGB chassis provided safe and predictable handling, through ageing lever arm dampers at the front and half-elliptic leaf springs at the rear. Steering was rack-and-pinion, with disc brakes at the front and drums at the back. A fibreglass 'works' hard-top made for draught-free winter motoring.

For long-distance events such as the Tour de France, the works MGBs were fitted with streamlined noses to improve aerodynamics. The Paddy Hopkirk/Andrew Hedges car pictured here finished nineteenth in the 1964 Le Mans 24-Hours, and was timed at 139mph (224km/h) on the Mulsanne straight. Apart from its track appearances, the MGB was also rallied occasionally and Donald and Erle Morley's works car took the GT category and finished seventeenth overall in the 1964 Monte Carlo Rally.

The works MGB of Paddy Hopkirk/Andrew Hedges finished eleventh in the 1965 Le Mans 24 Hours. It covered 2,357 miles (3,794km), averaging 98.2mph (158.1 kmh) some 548 miles (883km) fewer than the winning Ferrari 250LM of Rindt/Gregory.

This Grand Tourer pre-dated the factory-produced MGB GT by about a year. Created by Belgian coachbuilder Jacques Coune of Brussels in 1964, the Berlinette *was based on a standard roadster body, with fibreglass roof and back end, and a steel box section welded between the rear wheelarches to provide rigidity. In all, Coune built fifty-eight* Berlinettes.

MGC

Largely underestimated and misunderstood, the MGC was an excellent long-distance cruiser – albeit a thirsty one – with a top speed of 120mph (195km/h). It was eagerly anticipated as the successor to the mighty Austin-Healey 3000, a role it could never fulfil without considerable development. A couple of international racing successes tantalizingly hinted at wasted potential. Later cars were much improved, but the MGC was not a success in sales terms and the new British Leyland regime ditched it; 4,527 roadsters were built between 1967 and 1969.

Outwardly similar to the regular MGB GT, apart from taller 15in wheels and bonnet bulges, the MGC GT used the 2,912cc straight-six C-series engine, which developed 145bhp at 5,250rpm. Redesigned independent front suspension was by torsion bars and telescopic dampers, but because of the extra weight up front, it tended to understeer. Only 4,449 GTs were produced.

The MGC GT is a handsome grand touring car by any standards – with fresh air accessed via an optional full-length Webasto sunroof – but children can only be carried on the rear bench seat with the front seats fully forward – as seen here, with the driver hard up against the steering wheel. When unoccupied the rear seat folds flat to provide additional luggage space.

The MGB engine lent itself to competition preparation, and was campaigned in varying states of tune. This engine, in crackle black finish, has a fly-off oil filler cap and breathes through a twin choke 40DCOE Weber carburettor, and the heater has been removed for lightness.

Logically, the MGC's cast-iron 2,912cc in-line six extends further forward than the B's four-cylinder motor and it develops 145bhp at 5,250rpm, driving through a four-speed manual gearbox with optional overdrive or Borg Warner 35 three-speed automatic box. The C's bonnet-bulge is necessary to clear the front of the rocker cover and the blister on the left-hand-side accommodates the front SU's dash-pot.

Decline and Renaissance

With a cosmetic facelift in Autumn 1969, the Midget Mk III became the G-AN5 type, sharing its grille configuration with the Sprite as well as having the ubiquitous Rostyle wheels and BLMC badges on its flanks. From 1972 to 1974 the rear wheelarches were semi-circular in shape.

A number of 'facelifts' were visited on the MGB in its Mk II guise, none of which improved on the original design. The MGB GT in its final chrome-bumper format – 1972 to 1974 – had a plain mesh grille with a proper chrome surround, but was constrained to run on unattractive Rostyle wheels.

These unsightly growths were described as 'energy-absorbing over-riders,' and were fitted by British Leyland to comply with United States 5mph (8km/h) impact regulations. A former 'Miss MG', Pat Powell, was on hand to help sell the idea, but they had no option in fact, since two thirds of BL's sports-car production was exported to the States during 1972–1973.

Strangely for a BL press picture, this 1975 Midget engine bay shows clear evidence of painted-over corrosion along the scuttle and bulkhead seams. The point of the picture is that from late 1974, the Midget received the 1500 Triumph Spitfire engine, hence the Rover-Triumph badge on the air filter.

By 1980 the Midget's days were numbered and, like the MGB, it had suffered the indignity of having its suspension jacked up to meet headlight height regulations, and the rubberized girders which were necessary to pass further US crash-test requirements.

This Golden Jubilee Special was finished in an approximation of British Racing Green with gold striping to commemorate the fiftieth anniversary of MG – although by 1975 when it appeared, the company was in its fifty-second year. A limited edition of 750 units was produced.

As a company MG was closed down in 1980 and the very last MGBs were called LE – for Limited Edition – and the 420 roadsters were painted bronze, the 580 GTs finished in pewter; the add-on bumper arrangement was augmented by an air dam.

While the MGB's mechanical specification – and therefore performance – remained largely unchanged from 1967, the exterior underwent regressive facelifts. The interior fared little better, although in 1977 the fascia was revised and the seats covered in garish stripes.

Not Montego Bay, although British Leyland was 'all at sea' over the axing of Abingdon. The possibility of an Aston Martin take-over in 1981 was lost because BL refused to relinquish the right to the MG name, which Austin Rover Group Ltd went on to use on family cars such as the Montego and Metro. Apologists argue that the Montego Turbo was in its day as competent as the ZA Magnette, but it had absolutely nothing to do with Abingdon.

First shown at the 1985 Frankfurt Show – and seen here at Earls Court – the EX-E prototype was styled by Rover Group's own design team, then under Roy Axe, and was built to accept the 250bhp Metro 6R4 engine, but never progressed beyond the show-car stage.

MG club racing is as keenly contested as ever, with classic machinery providing many treats for the enthusiast. Here, one of the enduring names of MGB competition, Barry Siddery-Smith, gets his Brown & Gammons sponsored B off to a sideways start at a wet Cadwell Park.

The engine compartment of the Group B Metro 6R4 showing the mid-mounted 2,495cc twin-turbo V6 Rover-derived power-plant, dry-sump lubrication tank and silencer arrangement.

The MGB RV8 of 1992 was something of an enigma. While it marked a welcome return of the traditional MG sports car, its suspension was not updated – other than by replacing the lever arm shockers at the front with coil springs and Koni dampers, and fitting anti-tramp rods to the axle – so its handling and roadholding could not match the 190bhp power produced by the 3.9-litre Rover V8 engine. The external facelift included plastic bumpers and side-skirts, Porsche 911 headlights and Metro door mirrors.

The MGF is powered by 1.8-litre Rover K-series twin-cam engine, which comes in two guises. The standard unit produces 118bhp, while variable valve timing boosts power to 143bhp.